I'm Not CRAZY,
but i might be a carrier

Infectious inspiration
from comedian
Charles Marshall

Kregel
Publications

I'm Not Crazy, But I Might Be a Carrier: Infectious Inspiration from Comedian Charles Marshall

Published by Kregel Publications, a division of Kregel, Inc., P.O. Box 2607, Grand Rapids, MI 49501.

Library of Congress Cataloging-in-Publication Data
Marshall, Charles W. (Charles Wesley)
I'm not crazy, but I might be a carrier : infectious inspiration from comedian Charles Marshall / by Charles W. Marshall.
    p.   cm.
1. Christian life—Miscellanea. 2. Wit and humor. I. Title.
BV4501.3.M2725   2008   248.402'07—dc22   2008006916

ISBN 978-0-8254-3419-8

Printed in the United States of America

08 09 10 11 12 / 5 4 3 2 1

To Laura, for all you are to me.
I love laughing with you.

Contents

Part 5: Psychosomatic (It's All in His Head)

Part 6: Fitness Fixation

Part 7: In-House Treatment

Part 8: Issues at Home

Part 9: Excessive Food Swings

Part 10: Holiday Blues

Part 11: Criminally Inane

Acknowledgments

Thanks to:

Jeanette Windle, for liking this little book and believing in it enough to bring it to the attention of Kregel.

My literary agent and friend, Chip MacGregor, who acts like he has nothing better to do than give me advice and assistance.

The good folks at Kregel, for welcoming me into their family and enthusiastically adopting this project.

Mom and Dad, who taught me to laugh at life and love the people around me.

My children, Faith and Wesley Marshall, who are a never-ending source of joy.

And to my best friend, partner, and wife, Laura Marshall. It is not an exaggeration to say that this book would never have come into being without her belief and support.

part 1
Delusional Obsessions

chapter 1

Going to the Dogs

My wife and I have been thinking about getting a dog, lately, and discussing what type we might get. For me, there is really only one possibility—and that, of course, is a real dog.

For the uninitiated, there are three basic types of dogs:

1. *Real dogs.* These are dogs as God originally made them—monstrous, made-for-the-outdoors hunting machines that are perfect for intimidating neighbors and attracting lawsuits.

   The ownership rule for guys and dogs is simple: the bigger the dog, the cooler you look. Walk down the street with a Pekingese and you might as well be wearing a tutu.

   When you observe a man walking down the street with a massive real dog, his message to you is clear. "Yes, I'm overcompensating for my insecurities and lack of masculinity, but I've got a really big dog."

   Now that's the kind of attitude I can get behind.

2. *Mutant rat-dogs,* otherwise known as Chihuahuas. These poor creatures are the unintentional result of secret experiments conducted by the Mexican army in a failed attempt to create the ultimate weapon by cross-breeding bats and Great Danes. The only

surviving result of these experiments is a group of nervous, angry, little rat-dogs that have decided to take their revenge on humanity by being annoying on just about every level known to mankind.

If you are approached by one of these aberrations of nature, know that it despises you with a hatred rarely seen outside the Middle East, and that it won't hesitate to tear your ankles to shreds. These dogs are the piranhas of the canine world and would nuke mankind tomorrow if they thought they could get away with it. Under no circumstance should one of these animals be allowed to run for public office.

3. *Kitty-dogs*, which is every breed of dog that does not fall into one of the first two categories. I'm all in favor of this type of dog because, hey, girls have to have dogs too.

    The curse of the kitty-dog is that there are those who take a warped delight in dressing them up like people. Most dogs would rather be subjected to Mexican weapons experiments than go through this type of torture.

I cannot say this in strong enough terms: You should never, ever dress up your dog for any reason whatsoever. Take it from me—even if it were thirty below outside, your dog would rather die with dignity in his own fur coat than be seen in a little poochie parka.

If you dress up your dog, you need to know two things:

1. The rest of us are making fun of you behind your back.
2. Every day, your dog prays for a heaven where he gets to dress you up in humiliating costumes while he

and his doggie friends point at you and laugh for all eternity.

If you feel you absolutely must dress an animal, go dress one that at least has a chance of defending itself—like a cougar or a wolverine or a Chihuahua.

One of the most amazing things about the three dog types is that for every one of them, there is someone who likes that kind of dog. At this very moment, there are people risking the loss of fingers and eyes while they stroke their vicious little rat-dogs, all for the sake of love.

That's a mysterious kind of love, isn't it—the kind that embraces the unlovely, that sees through the imperfect and loves without regard?

Let's face it, the human heart isn't very attractive either. Every thought we have is consumed with self. If you peel away the layers of even our most noble deeds and acts of kindness, you will find thoughts that circle back to ourselves like homing pigeons. In our hearts, we are all mutant rat-dogs.

And yet God loves us.

In the Bible, you find that same theme of an indefatigable, undefeatable love reaching out to a vicious, ungrateful humanity over and over again. I've found it's a love well worth pursuing.

And so the great dog debate rages in my household, and I think my wife is coming around to my point of view. But if by chance you happen to see me in the neighborhood walking a Pekingese that is wearing a teeny hat and sundress, you may safely assume things did not go my way.

chapter 2

A Salute to Pants

It's that time of year again when it has become necessary for me to switch from shorts to pants, and I couldn't be happier. I had almost forgotten the comfort, warmth, and security that wearing pants provides. It's just like getting a hug of sunshine, but without the searing heat and life-threatening melanoma.

The reason I'm writing about pants, though, is to address a looming danger. In view of current global hostilities, it is only a matter of time before some nut somewhere learns how to make a bomb out of pants, and then the TSA agents out at the airport will start asking us to place our pants on the conveyor belt to be screened.

This is exactly how the revolution will begin, because under no circumstance will I willingly surrender my pants. It might get ugly. They might beat me. They might drag me off to jail, but, by jingo, I'll have my pants on.

My friends, we must not let them take our pants. Our civilization depends on it. Without pants, our society comes crashing down.

Just look at what happened to Rome. You may well argue that the Romans created a successful empire wearing togas (which, in the original language, translates "man-skirts"), but if that form of apparel was so great, why didn't their civilization last?

The answer is obvious. No pants. That's right. After they went prancing around in their togas for a few years, their enemies didn't take them seriously anymore. If you don't believe me, put on a dress, pick a fight with someone, and see what happens.

Even after the fall of Rome (and possibly well into the winter), their enemies were still snickering at them.

"And what of the Scots and their kilts?" you may ask.

No one can deny their smart fashion sense and style, but at the end of the day, they're still wearing skirts.

"But weren't the Scots fierce warriors at one time?" you ask.

Yes, admittedly they did well in a few battles in the distant past, but they're not exactly considered a major world power anymore, are they? It wasn't the Scots that pulled Europe out of that mess back in World War II, was it?

No sir. That's why the phrase "Don't worry, the Scots will defend us" has never gained popularity.

But it's not really the Scots' fault that they lost the struggle for world dominance. It's hard to concentrate on fighting when you're worried that your dress might fly up at any minute.

Recognition of the importance of pants goes back at least as far as Sun Tzu's *Art of War*: "All other factors being equal, the side wearing pants will always win the battle."

So, yes, I love pants. I maintain that pants are the ultimate clothing item, the pinnacle of perfection in apparel. If mankind had not been in the habit of going *au naturel* in Eden, I believe that God would have created pants on the eighth day—and then may have thrown in chocolate too, as a bonus.

Have you ever stopped to reflect on the wonder that is pants? I'm getting so emotional about this subject, I'm moved to render a poem.

Ode to Pants

Oh, the wonder that is pants!
   It's hard to imagine a circumstance
In which I'd not want pants in this world
   Unless, of course, I were a girl
So, hail to you, noble pair of jeans!
   To slacks and trousers and dungarees
I now salute you with poetic device
   And pray you're worn in paradise.

Yes, I am passionate about my pants, but what's wrong with having a little passion in your life? I get excited when I encounter things that work for me, and I want to let the world know about them.

That's the way I feel about the good things God has done in my life. When I think of all his miracles, and the ways he has blessed me, it's hard not to get excited; and sometimes, if I'm not real careful, it leaks out a tad.

I think this might not be an altogether unhealthy process because it has a tendency to encourage others and let them know that God is still active on this planet. One of the central themes of the Bible is that God is very much interested in mankind and is still very relevant in our world.

That thought encourages me and gives me hope, because I know that in whatever circumstance I may find myself, God will be there—even if, heaven forbid, I find myself out at the airport, waiting for my pants to come down the conveyor belt out of the X-ray machine.

Let's just pray that the pants bomb is never perfected.

chapter 3

Sharing My Faith with Aliens

The other day, I was watching a TV program about crop circles and UFOs. That very same night, I wound up being abducted by aliens. I know. What a coincidence. What're the chances, right?

Anyway, after I was brought aboard the spaceship, I underwent the prerequisite deep sinus-cavity probulation, which, it turns out, has nothing at all to do with scientific experimentation, but is just their way of saying "howdy-do" to strangers.

They were shocked and astounded to learn that we don't like to be probulated, in the same way some people are amazed when they learn that their house guests don't like to have the cocker spaniels jumping all over them when they come to visit.

Abductees who don't pass out from the probulation are always invited to have a cup of tea and sit down for a good chin wag with their hosts. (Aliens are excessively fond of British slang and culture.)

I don't remember a lot about the conversation, but I do remember learning that these aliens are not so far from here as we thought. It turns out they're from Quadrant B in the Zeron sector—or Canada, as we call it. They hang out in the thinly populated forest regions and are good friends with Bigfoot, whom they regard as something of a rock star.

I've printed what I remember of the conversation below.

ME: So what's up with all the crop circles?
ALIEN: That's just some of our kids doing graffiti. Believe
         me, it ticks us off just as much as it does you
         guys.
ME: So then, are they writing messages, or what?
ALIEN: Yeah, if you could call 'em that. Most of the time
         it's just stuff like "Zaydor Rules!" or "Zoron loves
         Kathy." Stuff like that.
ME: Man, that's disappointing. What about those
         mysterious lines and drawings down in Peru?
         We've always thought that was you guys . . .

The alien leaned over and in a conspiratorial tone told me
that he couldn't really comment on that subject because there
were several lawsuits pending. Then he stood up abruptly
and started running around the room screaming, "Death to
attorneys! Death to attorneys!" I suddenly felt a warm sense
of camaraderie with the alien and realized our two species
have more in common than I had originally thought.

Just as I was beginning to think our conversation was
going nowhere, he asked me why we humans were so confounded (yes, he said "confounded") obsessed with aliens
and the like.

I told him I believe it is because we humans suffer a fun-
damental disconnectedness from God, which often leads
to our searching blindly for that mysterious missing bond.
Some people seek to heal their internal disconnect with
fame and fortune; some try achievement; others even try
hollow religion, but none of these things work. Then I mentioned that we have a book called the Bible that explains all
of this and even recommends a solution.

At this, the alien nodded sagely and asked if I would like another probulation.

Then, a dozen aliens jumped out from behind curtains, laughing and cackling in the way that only aliens and Canadians can, yelling, "You've been Zorked!" Apparently I had been the guest on an alien reality show that airs on obscure planets at the far end of the galaxy and also on the FOX network.

This turn of events was terribly annoying because I felt the conversation was finally getting somewhere. I have concluded that, in general, aliens are pretty shallow and have more spare time on their hands than, say, your typical federal employee or Christian comedian.

Of course, it could be that this entire conversation, indeed this entire chapter, is a complete fabrication, the fictitious result of an overactive and fevered imagination.

[*Dramatic pause.*]

Or is it?

[*Cue* Twilight Zone *music.*]

chapter 4
The Dangers of Sauntering

A s one for whom observation is not only a way of life but also a source of income, I feel it is incumbent upon me to report an alarming, and I believe dangerous, trend in our society today.

I am convinced that sauntering is once again on the rise.

Historical note: As you'll no doubt remember, sauntering enjoyed its heyday back in the mid-1920s, when gambling, moonshine, and gangstering were all in vogue. Coincidence? I think not.

In fact, sauntering can now be linked directly to most of the world's major catastrophes, including rap music and Jessica Simpson's acting career.

As it turns out, the actual cause of the Great Depression was not the crash of the stock market in 1929, as was originally thought. No, it was the culmination of a decade of folks sauntering around when they should have been at work. It is widely held in some circles that were it not for sauntering, the Great Depression might have been only the Mildly Bummed Out.

Sauntering was virtually stamped out in the mid-1940s by the no-nonsense, tougher-than-nails World War II generation when they discovered that none other than Adolf Hitler, in addition to his other atrocities, was a known saunterer. Some prominent historians now believe that the goose step was merely a clumsy Bavarian imitation of sauntering.

Everywhere I go these days, it seems there is someone sauntering right in front of me, seemingly with all the time in the world, and usually when I'm running way behind schedule. Without exception, these people haunt small corridors while carrying large packages, engaged in deep conversations with their slow-moving, sauntering friends. Meanwhile, I'm running back and forth behind them, looking for that elusive gap that will allow me to pass and get where I'm going.

But perhaps you think I'm being too harsh. What harm is there in a little sauntering? The danger is that it won't stop there. First we accept sauntering as an allowable standard, and then, before you know it, people will start wanting to mosey. After that, rambling will become fashionable, and then strolling can't be far behind. Finally, the entire human race will meander to a halt, not unlike the ancient race known as the Meanderthals.

Additional historical note: The Meanderthals were a little-known offshoot of the much more popular and often show-offy Neanderthals. The Meanderthals ultimately failed to distinguish themselves as a race, though, meandering pointlessly through history and, quite literally, never really took off.

The Meanderthals' motto is thought by some scholars to have been, "Oom kooma ba jowie," which translates literally, "My shoelaces are untied."

The problem with most saunterers is they don't even know they're guilty of the crime. In order to find out whether you are indeed, um . . . rapid-movement challenged, just answer this simple questionnaire:

1. Do you frequently find yourself eyeing your grandma's walker and saying things like, "Hey, that's a nice walker. Does that come in different colors?"
2. Are the words "United States Government" or "State of . . ." printed on the issuer portion of your paycheck?
3. Are you presently incarcerated?
4. Are you a citizen of any formerly Soviet-controlled country?

If you replied affirmatively to any of the above questions, you are very likely a saunterer.

When I'm dancing behind these saunterers like a four-year-old who has to go to the bathroom, I find that the strangest thing happens. From somewhere deep inside, I hear the words, "My times are in your hands" (Psalm 31:15).

Suddenly, I remember that all of my life, including my schedule, is in God's hands. I remember that surrendering myself to him means submitting my schedule, my priorities, and even my anxieties to his care. It's amazing how much easier life's annoyances are to bear when you're submitted to the Lord's will.

This revelation, of course, translates into my having a much more relaxed attitude. I used to harbor rather harsh feelings toward saunterers, but now I'm in favor of more lenient prison sentences for them. See how God's grace is permeating my life?

chapter 5

Inner-Office Conflict When You Work by Yourself

I recently hired someone to help out with the administrative chores in my office. It's great to finally have some help, because for the great majority of my career, I have been the one and only employee of Charles Marshall, Inc. Just me, and only me, running the whole shebang.

But even though I have been both manager and employee for the past sixteen years, don't think my company hasn't faced the same challenges as larger companies, such as the time we instituted Casual Dress Friday. Because the office dress code is already relaxed (I'm wearing sweats as I write this), the memo announcing Casual Dress Friday caused disastrous results. One employee, who shall remain nameless, took the memo literally, and wore a casual dress to work the very first Friday. After being disciplined by management, this employee wore his jammies the next Friday. Again, management was not amused.

We, like so many other companies, have also suffered our share of employee–management strife. The worst of it came when management launched a surprise drug testing program. Every employee was expected to participate, and no one was exempt. The staff was surprised and offended when they came in to work one Monday morning only to learn that they were expected to take a drug test. There was no forewarning at all, and this audacious move by management was not at all appreciated.

The staff's reticence to take the drug test aroused the suspicions of management, and accusations ensued. The staff was insulted, incensed, and threatened to walk out en masse. Fortunately, management took the lead by volunteering to go first, and this placated all but one employee, whom we haven't been able to get a decent day's work out of since.

The most severe problem came just last year when accusations were made of office theft. The conflict began when certain items in the office unaccountably disappeared. Nothing very valuable or important was taken, but an air of suspicion and distrust hung over the office for days. Tension was high and tempers flared. At one point, blows were actually exchanged and the police were called to break it up. No charges were filed, but there was a court-ordered psychiatric evaluation.

The whole matter was finally resolved when a memo was issued proclaiming complete amnesty for the thief if he would agree to return the missing items. The very next day, the items were returned, with no charges filed and no questions asked.

Things have since calmed down and one of the surprise benefits of having a new employee is that it seems to help keep everyone on their best behavior.

Conflict, it seems, is inevitable in this life, whether working with two hundred people or by yourself. Jesus knew all about conflict. It seems there was always someone who had a problem with the way he was doing something. Whether it was his healing on the Sabbath, letting his disciples pick grain on the Sabbath, or hanging out with so-called social undesirables, there was always somebody who had something negative to say about it.

One of the things that I really like about Jesus, though, is that he didn't let that conflict alter his vision or determine his direction. He didn't let others' opinions define his self-worth. Neither did he let conflict diminish his love for people. All that mattered to Jesus was his Father's opinion.

Adherence to God's will allows us to sail through the turbulence of conflict while retaining the inner peace of knowing that we're okay with the One that matters.

As for me, some say that being cooped up by oneself in a small office for extended periods of time will cause symptoms of dementia and multiple personality disorder, but I haven't found this to be true.

And to be honest, neither have I.

chapter 6

Coming to Terms with My Shortcomings

Okay, I'm not perfect, but do I have to keep being reminded? And why is it that our greatest strengths are also our greatest weaknesses? With me, it's (you guessed it) my mouth.

The other day, I was chatting with the carpet cleaning guy, who had come by to give me an estimate. He told me that before he started his own carpet cleaning business, he used to be a corporate litigator.

From my extensive research into the legal profession (i.e., reading John Grisham novels), I knew that being a corporate litigator takes a lot of moxie. You have to be an aggressive, in-your-face guy with teeth, who doesn't mind using them.

"Man, you have to have teeth to be in that profession!" I exclaimed.

Unfortunately, it was only then that I noticed that he, in fact, had no teeth. Not a one. You'd think I would have picked up on that sooner. It sure would have been handy.

At this point, although the day was a mild sixty-five degrees, I began sweating profusely. I think I may have blacked out for a moment, because when I came to, I found myself babbling inanely about the nobility of practicing law, or some other such nonsense, in my attempt to salvage this plane-crash situation. I finally dug my way out by buying the extra-super-deluxe carpet cleaning package.

Sometimes I find it amazing that God has allowed me, with all my shortcomings, to serve him in comedy ministry. But the Bible is littered with examples of unlikely candidates that the Lord chose to use. Just look at the guys Jesus picked as his disciples. Most of them were definitely rough around the edges, but Jesus saw something in them that others didn't.

The one I've been thinking about lately is Thomas. Remember "Doubting Thomas"? He's the guy who essentially said to Jesus, "You're trying to tell me you're resurrected? Yeah, I'll believe that when I can actually touch the wounds that killed you" (King Charles Marshall Standard Revised Version).

Don't you find it just a touch odd that Jesus, who placed such a high premium on faith, chose Thomas? How many times were the disciples chided for a lack of faith, and yet Jesus picks a guy he knows is a pragmatic, gotta-see-it-for-myself kind of guy. Amazing! You'd think that he would be just the kind of person that might not fit into the organization.

But maybe Jesus saw hidden possibility in Thomas and granted him the grace to fulfill that potential.

God is still in the same business today. He takes the most unlikely people and uses them. Don't ever let anyone tell you that God cannot use your life. Don't ever believe that amazing things cannot be achieved through you as you surrender yourself to God's will.

So, find out what God wants you to do, and go out and take a bite outta life. Just make sure you put your teeth in first.

part 2
Social-Paths

chapter 7

Unexplored Relationship Markets

In the spirit of love and charity, I thought I might tackle a problem that is plaguing many single, middle-aged guys all over the country. These gentlemen are scratching their heads, wondering why they aren't attracting the good-looking, younger women that they used to.

Yep, it's a real mystery all right, and I'm here to help.

This is a tough concept to communicate to men, so I thought I might reveal the answer to this enigma in a way most men can understand: business-speak.

Remember twenty or thirty years ago when you first went on the market (started dating)? This was your IPO (Initial Public Offering) and your stock debuted at an all-time high.

You were a hot commodity and trading was vigorous and steady. Investors (womenfolk) couldn't get enough of you. You thought the demand would never end, but unfortunately, this was as high as your stock would ever climb.

Yes, my friend, the sad truth is that, over the years, the value of your stock has—and I want to put this delicately—well, it's just plummeted. That's right. It has taken a dive off the high board.

Tanked. Crashed and burned.

Collapsed. Given up the ghost.

How did this happen? Simply put, first inflation set in

(weight gain) and then recession ensued (hair loss), resulting in a massive stock devaluation (you are now invisible to
babes).

But do not despair, my bald, chubby, middle-aged buddy,
for I bring you good news and great hope. All is not lost.
Even though you have certainly lost your primary market,
there are several niche markets you might have overlooked:

1. *Jail brides.* Guys in prison are always getting married.
    I know this is true. I saw it on TV. Apparently, pris-
    oners are in big demand. This means there has got to
    be a woman out there somewhere desperate enough
    to want even you. All you need to do to get one of
    these babes is go to jail. The longer your term of im-
    prisonment, the better your chances of finding the
    gal of your dreams.

2. *Golden girls.* Forget rejection and heartache. Say
    good-bye to loneliness. The seventy-years-plus babes
    think you're hot stuff! In a marvelous turn of events,
    you are now the eye candy. Senior single chicks are
    champing at the bit for a young guy like you (defined
    as any man without a pacemaker).

    Your new golden girlfriend will enjoy showing
    you off when you visit her at the rest home, and all
    her friends will absolutely drool over you, or perhaps
    they will just drool in general. Nevertheless, much
    drooling will take place when you visit your new
    girlfriend.

    On a typical date, you will engage in romantic ac-
    tivities such as doing crossword puzzles, comparing
    medications, and dozing off in front of the television.
    What a hoot that will be!

3.   *Gold diggers.* It's amazing how much better looking a guy is when he has megabucks. Trust me, if Donny Trump worked in the next cubicle and drove an '84 Escort, he wouldn't be dating supermodels. No sir, if you want to achieve a whole new level of attractiveness, go get yourself a billion bucks or so. It's the most often overlooked makeover.

Let's face it; it's tough to find love in this world. Our society is not particularly kind to those of us who don't look like movie stars.

When you're tempted to define your self-worth by the world's standards, remember Psalm 36:7: "How priceless is your unfailing love! Both high and low among men find refuge in the shadow of your wings."

I like that "both high and low among men" part. To me, that means God's love extends beyond the superficial, and our value to him doesn't wear out, grow old, or lose its hair. Isn't it good to know that your stock will never lose its value in God's eyes?

As I wrap up this chapter, it suddenly occurs to me how fortunate I am to be married. I think we can all agree that, if I weren't, it's a certainty I'd be trolling the halls of some nursing home, looking for a golden girlfriend of my own.

chapter 8

Dysfunctional Computer Relationships

I'm thinking about breaking up with my computer.

This is actually my second computer. My first computer was an older model with granite components made by the Flintstone Corporation. It worked fine unless I quit pedaling.

I've been seeing the computer I have now for about three years, and a more dysfunctional relationship one could not imagine. I can't stand my computer, but I can't live without it either.

The problem we're having lately is that it works fine when I don't need it, but whenever there is something important to be done, it decides to check out on me.

I know that this is very likely my computer's cry for attention. It knows that I'm losing interest in it, so it constantly makes pathetic attempts to get my attention. "Um, excuse me, Sweetie, I've got updates. Would you like to install them now?"

This, of course, is a diabolically manipulative question, because if I say yes, then my computer is tied up for fifteen minutes while I wait for the updates to be installed. If I say no, then the computer crashes, blames me for not updating it when it asked me to, and we get into this huge fight. It's a no-win situation.

On top of my twisted relationship with my computer lies the additional layer of dysfunctionality that my Internet Service Provider brings to the table. Unfortunately, I can't mention their name for fear of legal action, so let's just say the name of the company is—Monstrous Organization Repeatedly Obstructing Net Service, or MORONS for short. Having MORONS is like being in a relationship with someone who never does what you want them to unless you don't need them to do it anymore.

My typical conversation with my MORONS program usually goes something like this:

ME: I'd like to check my e-mail.
MORONS: Yes, I'll be with you in a moment, but right now
            I'm busy frustrating the other two trillion people
            dumb enough to use my services.
ME [*five minutes later*]: I really, really would like to check
            my e-mail now.
MORONS: I have no doubt that you would like to check
            your e-mail, and I'm enjoying your aggravation
            immensely. Please, stand by.
ME [*twenty minutes later*]: Never mind. I can't wait the
            rest of my life just to check my e-mail. Abort the
            process.
MORONS: Oh, you wanted to check your e-mail? I had no
            idea. Let's see now . . . nope, you don't have a
            thing. That'll be $25.

I know what you're thinking: If I have so much trouble with MORONS, why don't I just dump them? Because it's impossible, that's why. MORONS is like the Mob. You never get out. Just try to stop the service, and they lure you back by giving you months and months of free service—a tactic I always fall for.

ME: I want to close my account because you guys stink.

MORONS: How about this instead: You agree to stay with us, and we'll give you even more of the lousy service that you despise, at absolutely no charge.

ME: Wow! What a great deal! I'll take it!

It's true, though, that a computer is a machine and machines have problems. It's part of life. When you stop having problems, you need to check your pulse, because you may not be on planet Earth anymore.

I think this is because we're living in Plan B. Plan A involved a garden, an almost-all-you-can-eat buffet, and a very relaxed dress code. That plan went awry, and here we are in Plan B.

One of my favorite Plan B verses is Psalm 34:15: "The eyes of the LORD are on the righteous and his ears are attentive to their cry."

I like it because it reminds me that God didn't abandon mankind, even in our folly, and he remains ready to come to our aid in the most trying of times—such as tragedy, illness, and distress—or in the most ridiculous of situations, such as computer relationship problems.

I do admit that I'm partially to blame for my computer problems. I realize now that I shouldn't have begun a relationship so soon after breaking up with my old computer. Those rebound relationships never work. Is there such a thing as human/computer relationship counseling?

chapter 9

Marital Tips for the Groom-to-be

A friend of mine recently told me he was engaged. Because he's never lived with a woman, I told him he's going to need to buy a few things that he hasn't used before, such as household cleaning supplies and furniture not made out of old milk crates.

After our conversation, I felt bad because I realized I had offered him no real insight into the mysteries of matrimonial union. So, in order to correct this oversight, I offer the following, heretofore undisclosed, observations to all young men contemplating walking the aisle.

Revelatory Marriage Fact No. 1. Getting married is like getting a free memory upgrade. As a man, your hard drive was filled up long ago with important stuff like sports scores and movie trivia, but women, for some inexplicable reason, have tons of extra storage capacity that is yours for the asking.

As a married man, you may feel free to store stuff on her hard drive that you think you might need later but don't want to bother remembering yourself.

"Wow, this is a great hamburger. Remind me to order this the next time we're here."

This is a tremendous resource that you will learn to thoroughly exploit. You will frequently find yourself asking her such questions as, "Honey, what's the name of that song that

I like?" or "What're the names of those people that we're friends with?" or "What's my middle name?" The possibilities are as exciting as they are endless.

Wives are also frightfully good at remembering superfluous information, like the names of your children and their dates of birth. All you will need to do is show up for your kid's birthday party and act like you know what's in the present he's opening.

Revelatory Marriage Fact No. 2. When you get married, you will develop noncommunication skills. God made women such that they use about three times the number of words as any man in one day.

How is a guy supposed to interact with such a creature? In short, you're not. Even attempting such a thing could almost instantaneously institutionalize you—or worse, turn you into a girl. Instead, you must develop the skill of tuning out your wife by converting the sound of her voice into white noise that you can easily ignore.

There is no way to instruct a young groom-to-be in this valuable art, but don't worry, it will just happen. It's a wondrous, mystical thing like falling in love, discovering a new kind of power tool, or getting a bite on your hook. You must relax and let it come to you. Rest assured, though, that one day you will be able to ignore your wife with the best of us.

When ignoring your wife, it is important to remember to evade detection by maintaining a semblance of conversation. Don't try anything fancy at first, or you'll get busted for sure. Just a simple "Hmm?" or "Uh-huh" muttered occasionally will suffice. After a while, you can graduate to "You don't say" and "How about that."

If she ever asks you, "What do you mean by that?" know that you have ventured too far and have officially blown your cover. You might as well start learning to "share your feelings" and "have conversations." [Shudder.]

I recently read about a guy in Des Moines who started cutting coupons and getting manicures as a direct result of having conversations with his wife.

True story.

Getting married can be a little scary, because you're venturing into uncharted waters. You're transitioning into a new stage of your life and you don't know what to expect.

The important thing to remember when going through any change in life is that God's love never changes. Nor is he ever far from you. Whatever awaits you on the other side of any change you encounter, you can count on God to not only walk with you through the transition, but also to be with you on the other side of it.

So I would encourage all you soon-to-be-married young men out there to embrace the change in your life. Oh, and you might also want to purchase a clothes hamper. I think you'll find that you are no longer able to use the kitchen table as a dirty clothes receptacle.

chapter 10

Dancing with the Stars —or with Natasha and Bob, Anyway

Not long ago, my wife and I took a ballroom dance class. I know it's wrong and I'm not proud of it. I'm just saying we did it but have since gotten our lives right with God again.

Signing up for dance lessons was very difficult for me, because I've just really never been able to figure out the point of dancing. Especially if you're single. Could there be a worse activity for two people considering a relationship with each other?

"Hi! My name's Frank. I will now gyrate my body in the most unfavorable and disagreeable fashion so that you may determine whether or not you think I'm a good long-term relationship risk." It just doesn't make sense.

So, my wife signs us up for dance lessons sponsored by our public school's Continuing Education Program, which means the same thing in my neighborhood as it does in yours: quality, excellence, and teachers who couldn't get a full-time gig.

Our teacher, whom I'll call Natasha because I've forgotten her real name, is a pleasant older lady who speaks what little English she knows in a thick Russian accent. She has been teaching dance since Moses was fished out of the Nile, but still dances like a fawn on a spring morning. That is to say, she dances in jerky, spasmodic motions, like someone trying to learn to use her legs for the first time. No, I only jest. She dances beautifully, but unfortunately possesses no actual teaching ability.

When my wife and I were learning the waltz, any question I'd ask Natasha would inevitably result in loud clapping in my face, accompanied by the words, "ONE two three, ONE two three. See? Is easy! No problem. ONE two three!"

Yes, that clears everything right up. Thanks.

Our teacher's dancing assistant, whom I'll call Bob because that's his name, also dances like a dream—by which I mean everything is out of place and nothing makes sense. Once again, I kid. His dancing is also superb.

Bob is roughly forty pounds overweight, but he doesn't know it because no one has told him. So he wears a skin-tight, white T-shirt that resembles sprayed-on latex, which is not very flattering, but nobody has told him that either. Bob has tattoos all over his arms and sports a foot-long, solid white ponytail, which rounds out his I-teach-dance-when-I'm-out-on-parole look.

From what I can tell, Bob's primary responsibilities seem to include periodically dancing with the women in the class while scolding them about the sin of not following the man while he's leading.

Finally, a candidate I can get behind.

After a while, Bob would run out of steam, relinquish his partner, and then hover longingly around the other couples, hoping that someone would ask him something so he could cut in and berate another woman mercilessly.

About three-fourths of the way through each class, Natasha and Bob would typically give up on their slow-witted, clumsy students and start gliding around the floor like Fred and Ginger. The rest of us would then look for our opportunity to slip out of the room without getting caught, like restaurant patrons trying to skip out on the check.

It feels good to get this all off my chest. The Bible says to "confess your sins to each other" (James 5:16), but it's amazing how seldom we actually do it.

Maybe it's hard to be vulnerable with each other because we're afraid of what will happen if we are. Experience has taught us that honest confession might bring ridicule, criticism, and gossip.

Maybe it would be easier for us to confess our shortcomings and failures if we adopted an attitude of grace and cultivated a culture of mercy. In a fallen world, it takes no talent to point out everything that's wrong. It takes humility, however, to see God at work, even in the midst of disappointment and chaos.

So don't think too harshly of me for my ballroom dancing foibles. Instead, start praying for me right now. I just noticed my wife looking at the fall Ballroom Dancing II schedule.

chapter 11

Misled by the Love Songs of My Youth

My concept of love was messed up very early in life by television. I remember watching *The Monkees* on Saturday mornings as Peter, Michael, Davy, and Micky sang their songs and got chased around by beautiful girls. Somewhere in the back of my foggy little mind, I figured that this must be the preferred method of romantic interaction between a man and a woman. To this day, whenever my wife says something romantic to me, I start running around the house singing "The Last Train to Clarksville." It's a miracle we ever had kids.

Of course, the love songs I heard growing up didn't help either. I used to love to sing along to Eddie Rabbit's "Step by Step." The words that Eddie croons in this beloved ballad sound like great advice, unless of course you analyze the words.

"First step, ask her out and treat her like a lady."

Great advice. Women love this kind of stuff, but this is definitely the last time in the song you should take Eddie's counsel.

"Second step, tell her she's the one you're dreaming of."

This is where the song starts going awry. Most girls get

creeped out when guys tell them they've been dreaming about them on the first date.

"Thanks for going out with me, Betty. I've been dreaming about you for the past five years." Tell a girl this and you're one step away from a restraining order.

"Third step, take her in your arms and never let her go."

Now, this is just against the law. You can't even do this if you're married to the girl. Try it and you'll have the police surrounding your house. The law takes a dim view of this behavior, and you won't be scoring any points with the lady either.

"Don't you know that step by step, you'll win her love."

No, follow this advice, and step by step you're going to prison.

God's love isn't as hard to figure out, though. Some would tell you that God's love is unfathomable, but I believe that even though it's deep and hard to comprehend, it is apparent to those who have eyes to see.

The challenge in a fallen world is to find God amidst the chaos and pain, and to realize that he's on our side and passionately desires our good. The Bible says, "Blessed are the pure in heart, for they will see God" (Matthew 5:8).

The atheist tells me that every little occurrence of good in my life is merely a coincidence. He would have me believe that goodness is a random product of chance. But I can't help but notice that I have more of these coincidences in my life when I pray. The good news is that the God I've experienced—the God of the Bible—is alive and relevant in today's world.

Chapter 12
Kiss-Jeep

I don't know if you're aware of it, but I'm the guy who invented Kiss-Jeep. There are some parts of the country where Kiss-Jeep hasn't caught on yet, so let me explain.

Let's say you're driving down the road with your loved one(s). The first one in the car that spots a Jeep Wrangler (Jeep Cherokees don't count), yells "Kiss-Jeep!" and receives a kiss from the other party.

(Note to guys: This game should not be played when it's just you and your male friends in the car. Once you go down that road, then the next thing you know, you're all crying, sharing your feelings, and shopping together. You don't want to open that door.)

Why only Wranglers? I like 'em. I might want one some day. Some have advanced the theory that this is a symptom of a rapidly approaching mid-life crisis. Be that as it may, that's the vehicle you use for the game, and that's that.

Now I realize that this whole thing sounds a bit mushy and, well, stupid, but I had to invent this game as a defense against Punch-Bug.

I first heard of Punch-Bug about six or seven months ago. I was driving around with someone when suddenly they yelled, "Punch-Bug!" while simultaneously reaching over and whomping me on the arm. When I demanded an explanation, they looked at me with that look of mingled pity and disbelief that, if it were spoken, would sound like, "What a moron." It turns out that Punch-Bug has been around since the Garden of Eden and is played with Volkswagen Beetles and punching, rather than Wranglers and kisses.

This is an incredible concept to me—that there is actually a circumstance where it's not only okay to hit someone, but it's considered a good thing.

Amazing! I could've been assaulting people all my life and getting away with it, had I just known. I wonder now if there are other crimes one may commit and get away with if one knows the right thing to say. You see a nice car, yell, "Steal-Mercedes!" hop in and drive off. What a world!

So I hear about this Punch-Bug thing, go home, tell my wife, and before you can say "black and blue," we're driving down the road knocking the fool out of each other. After a while, I realized that she's much better at this than I am, because while I'm driving and looking at the road, traffic signals, speedometer, etc., the only activity she's engaged in is spotting Volkswagens and hitting me. She's a very competitive woman.

Seeing I was getting nowhere with this, I expanded the rules to include Slap-Van, Pinch-Truck, Hair-Yank-Import and Gouge-18-Wheeler. Even so, she soon caught on and was beating me senseless.

That's when I had my Kiss-Jeep brainstorm. I thought, *Which would be better—being punched or being kissed by one's sweetheart?* Hmmm. (Oddly enough, I can actually name some couples that would choose the punching.)

Now, because my eyes are automatically drawn to any Wrangler on the road, I'm spotting them left and right and having the time of my life! But the cool thing about Kiss-Jeep is, even when you lose, you win. Cool, huh?

Which gets me to my point, and that is: If you don't like the game, either change the rules or play a different game. I wonder if that might be what it means in Romans 12:2 when it says, "Do not conform any longer to the pattern of this world, but be transformed by the renewing of your mind. Then you will be able to test and approve what God's will is—his good, pleasing and perfect will."

Every day we're bombarded with ideologies and standards that we didn't choose. We're told that to be loved and/or accepted, we must have a certain look, wear a particular style of clothes, drive a nice car, live in a nice house.

We're told that sex outside of marriage is normal, that substance abuse is a right, that right and wrong are relative, and that faith is archaic. We must be socially conscious, environmentally sensitive, and politically correct.

We find ourselves in the middle of a game that we can't hope to win, and the funny thing is, a lot of us (yes, even us Christians) don't even question the game. We just jump in and try to compete.

But here's an idea for you: What if, instead of playing this game, we measured our actions, values, and standards, not according to popular opinion, but by the Bible? What if we looked at our lives and measured our thoughts and attitudes, not by what the media or even our friends say, but rather by what God says?

Why keep playing a game that God never intended for us, only to get beaten up? What if we chose to change the rules and play a different game rather than trying to hit harder and quicker than everyone else? What if we invested ourselves in a kingdom that is to come, instead of a system that will one day pass away?

In the meantime, you can keep playing Punch-Bug if you

want. Me? I'm keeping both hands on the wheel and my eyes on the road.

Oh, and I might keep an eye out for the occasional Wrangler here and there.

part 3
He-Manic
Depressive
Behavior

chapter 13

Defining the Rules of Manhood

In these confusing days of changing mores and shifting values, I thought it might be valuable for my male readers if I took a moment to review the four basic rules for manly men. (Women are also invited to listen in.)

Rule No. 1. A man must never talk about, mention, or otherwise refer to the subject of pants to another man. It's okay for women to talk about clothes—anybody's clothes, in any context whatsoever. But for a man to mention the subject of pants to another man, well, it just makes everybody feel awkward and uncomfortable.

There are no exceptions to this rule (unless you're writing a book chapter, of course). Such unacceptable phrases would include:

"Hey Frank, how do you like my new pants?"

"Wow! Those are nice pants."

See how awkward and uncomfortable that makes you feel?

And there is no situation in which this rule may be broken. Not even, "Um, buddy? Your pants just caught fire," is acceptable. Trust me, a man would much rather find out his pants are on fire himself than hear it from another guy.

Rule No. 2. Never talk to other men in the public restroom. The standard is that a man is allowed only one verbal exchange at the sink, and only at the sink, and that can only be about sports or the sermon (if at church).

For example: "Good sermon today."

"Yeah, how 'bout them Packers?" is a more-than-adequate men's room conversation.

Rule No. 3. Never verbally share your feelings with another man. This is not to say you can't share your feelings for him—just not verbally. He will appreciate it much more if you do one of the following:

1. Whack him on the back
2. Punch him on the shoulder
3. Nod

For a man to do all three at once is the highest form of manly man affection.

Rule No. 4. Never share your feelings about another man's pants in the men's restroom. Going into a men's room and saying something like, "Dude, let me tell you how I feel about your pants!" might just cause both parties irreparable damage in the community of manly men.

I should also point out that real men (and real women too, for that matter) seek the Lord and trust in Him. The Bible records a question that Jesus' disciples asked him: "What must we do to do the works God requires?" Jesus answered, "The work of God is this: to believe in the one he has sent" (John 6:28–29).

There it is. No complicated rules. No stipulations. No confusion.

The foundation and beginning of any meaningful relationship is trust. I believe God passionately desires to communicate that he can be trusted—with our families, our finances, and even our souls.

It isn't easy figuring out all the rules of this world, but don't you just love the idea of a God who is more concerned about relationships than rules?

chapter 14

Tricks for Dodging Traffic Tickets

E lection Day. What an exciting concept! To be the one chosen, to be the one selected of all the contenders. Of course, that's not always a good thing.

A couple of weeks ago, I was the one selected . . . for a traffic ticket. If you will allow me to express my sentiments about this incident by quoting Charlie Brown: "Aargh!"

For eighteen years, I've managed to avoid getting a traffic ticket. You know how I did it? My rule was simple: If ever pulled over, cry. That's it. And it works every time.

And I don't mean the sniffles either. I mean heartbreak, end of the world, bawling like a newborn crying. Now this technique is completely useless if you're a female. Cops have seen women cry before. But if you're a grown adult male, well, the policeman is so embarrassed for you that he practically sprints away after administering the sobriety test.

Now the trick is being able to conjure up that kind of emotion on the spot, which is difficult for most men. But for you guys who may need to try this, I offer the following tips:

1. Think about something that rips your heart out— like maybe your dog dying or losing your remote control.

2. Picture yourself in a hopeless situation, like being

3. Imagine yourself in a desperate, impossible struggle, like being trapped in a collapsed mine or having a conversation with your girlfriend about your relationship.

Are you starting to feel it?

So, you may be wondering, if this plan is so foolproof, Charles, why did you get tagged? Well, for some reason, this time I couldn't muster a tear. Not one. Nada.

I tried everything else. Charm. No good. Jokes. He wasn't amused. Appealing to his mercy. He was amused.

And, of course, I've had my share of counselors doling out bucketfuls of modern pseudowisdom like "it's all good" and "everything happens for a reason." Which, in addition to being annoying, is just plain wrong. It's not all good. Ever been to the DMV? Believe me, very little of that trip is going to be good. And "everything happens for a reason"? Well yeah, the purpose of my ticket was to spank me for going too fast and to help pay for the new courthouse.

It does help to turn to God's Word, though. Romans 8:28 says, "And we know that in all things God works for the good of those who love him, who have been called according to his purpose." Isn't that a lot more comforting than "it's all good"?

And it makes a lot more sense, too. In regard to traffic tickets and elections, it means that after doing our best to fulfill our responsibilities, we can trust God to care for his people in any circumstance.

So, the next time an election rolls around, here's hoping your guy wins (as long as he's my guy too!).

cast away from God's love for all eternity or having to take your wife shopping for shoes.

chapter 15

Manly Injuries

I 've been out of commission the past two or three weeks due to a broken toe I sustained while hiking in the Alaskan wilderness. My group was about fifteen miles away from camp when we were attacked by a twelve-foot Kodiak bear. I realized my group's only chance for survival was to use myself as a distraction while everyone else ran for safety. As I was charging the bear, I tripped over a twelve-foot Kodiak log and broke my toe.

This, of course, is an outright lie and we all know it. The log was thirteen feet if it was an inch. No, the whole story is a shameless fabrication, but it still sounds better than "I broke it climbing over a baby gate when I was racing for the phone," which is, in fact, what actually happened.

The main problem for a man with any visible injury is that sooner or later someone is going to ask him how it happened. Every guy knows there are both acceptable and unacceptable answers to this question. The criteria for acceptability pivot around the issue of manliness. Thus, any explanation with the words *Kodiak bear* is going to sound better than one with the words *baby gate*.

When confronted with the injury question, a man should only render a tough-guy answer. "I got wounded in a fight," or while playing a sport—or better yet, in a fight while playing a sport. Or even better, in a fight with a Kodiak bear while playing a sport.

Men should also note that any acceptable reason for an injury is immediately ruined if the injury happened while you were interacting with a woman.

"I broke my arm in a fight" sounds much better than "I broke my arm in a fight with a girl."

"I busted my ankle playing basketball" sounds immeasurably better than "I busted my ankle playing basketball with my eight-year-old niece."

I'll admit it is somewhat surprising to me that accidental gun injuries are considered by many to be acceptable manly injuries. Yes, in the case that you accidentally did yourself in ("I wonder if this trigger-thingy works?"), your friends would indeed talk in lowered tones about how manly you were.

After that, they would regale each other for hours with numerous stories of other not-so-bright things you did in your life. Meanwhile, you would have to spend all eternity explaining just how it was that you got to heaven ahead of schedule.

Please keep in mind that I didn't invent any of these rules for manliness. No, these are well-worn, time-tested laws of nature, just like gravity, lunar tides, and bad breath on the first date. These things are going to happen whether we like it or not.

Pain is a difficult thing to deal with, though. I remember being in the doctor's office as the nurse drew blood from my newborn daughter for some necessary tests. I gritted my teeth as my little girl's face registered her surprise and then pain, and I would have gladly traded places with her without a second thought.

I'm told this is not an uncommon sentiment among

parents. Over the years, I must have heard a half dozen stories of parents who drowned while attempting to save their children from a deadly undertow.

Such is the nature of love. Such is the nature of a parent's heart. Such is the nature of God's love for mankind. There is no pain you experience that the Lord is not aware of and does not care about. It is his nature to love you as his child.

And speaking of children, I have to go play basketball with my eight-year-old niece . . . I mean, um, with a Kodiak bear.

part 4

Dentally Challenged

chapter 16

Tough Guys Don't Need Novocain

I just got braces toward the end of February and had to have eight teeth pulled (that's right, eight!) in order to facilitate this process.

Of course, I was a tad nervous about having numerous teeth yanked out of my head, but I thought it might be helpful for my readers to see how a spiritually mature, professional Christian comedian handled the approach of a difficult trial, so that all might be strengthened through my exemplary example. To this end, I kept a journal of the days leading up to the extractions, which I have printed below.

February 1—Feeling good. Standing firm in my faith. So I'm getting eight teeth pulled. So what? Big deal. Little kids do it every day and aren't any worse for it. I can't believe I was scared at all. I scoff at pain. No, better yet, I laugh at pain. Ha!

February 3—Panicking. Blind terror. What was I thinking? I can't take pain. I cry whenever I get a splinter. This was a bad idea. I was presumptuous. God doesn't want me to have braces. I see that now. I'm calling the oral surgeon to cancel my appointment.

February 4—Foiled in my attempt to cancel my
appointment. Wife called oral surgeon's office
and told them to expect such a call from me.
When I called, they just laughed and told me
they'd see me on the seventeenth. Where's the
respect?

February 6—Feeling calmer today, although my wife said I
was crying for my mommy last night in my sleep,
begging her to "not let the bad man take my
toofies." This is a blatant lie, of course, intended
to humble me and make a point. The fact that
she made a recording of it changes nothing.

February 8—Booked flight to Venezuela for February 16.
Venezuela has no extradition treaty with the
United States, so I should be safe. I'll call my wife
a couple days after I arrive to let her know where
I am, and to tell her she's not the boss of me.

February 9—Drat! Wife found reservation and canceled it.
Must think of something else.

February 12—Sabotaged car. Don't know much about cars
but think this is a foolproof plan. Ha! Just let my
wife try and get me to the surgeon's office now!

February 13—Plan failed miserably. Car still works fine.
Apparently, taking ash tray didn't affect normal
operation of car. Getting discouraged. Running
out of options.

February 15—Locked myself in bathroom. Planned not to
come out for next two days but forgot to bring
food and television set. Got hungry after only
fifteen minutes. Went to get food. When I got
back, wife had disabled bathroom door lock.
Miserable. Consoled myself by eating entire box
of Ritz crackers.

February 16—Found out today my wife's been reading my
     journal. Dang! I should have anticipated this.
     Too late to formulate new plan. Doomed.
February 17—Morning of extractions. Terrified. Face
     numb. Have no feeling in my hands. Can't
     remember name. Haven't left house yet to go to
     oral surgeon's.
          Hard to breathe. Must concentrate so I can
     try passing out.
          Tried to pass out by holding breath.
     Unsuccessful. Tried hitting head on bathroom
     door to pass out. Also unsuccessful. Wife coming
     upstairs to get me and put me in car. Can't feel
     legs.
Fbluway 18888—heavyyy sedattid with paine piles, but I
     feeel grite. Pane faaar way n nutder countrrry.
     watchinm fummy talybishun shu cawlb "The
     nuse." Bury fummie. Tuk nuddter paene pil.
     Geeetin mor tireded. Kneed tu bezeele flammie
     diojf jdasdpofjp oppjdsfjapoje ijeogf aosj
     ijadoij . . .

Have you ever been scared? Sure you have. Everybody
gets scared now and then, but the secret to overcoming fear
is not trying to be tough, but realizing that you have a God
who is standing with you, come what may.

Isaiah 41:10 says, "Do not fear, for I am with you; do
not anxiously look about you, for I am your God. I will
strengthen you, surely I will help you, surely I will uphold
you with My righteous right hand" (NASB).

I've learned it's not whether or not you get scared, but
what you do with that fear. Will you let it overwhelm you
and prohibit you from achieving your potential, or will

you go forth, knowing that God is at your side, ready to strengthen and help you?

I do admit that it's a little disconcerting having braces at my age, though. All I need now is a few pimples and some high-waters, and I'll have the total middle-school makeover.

chapter 17

Getting In Touch with My Teeth

I recently had eight teeth pulled so that I could get braces. My initial reaction to this procedure was "Ahhh!" And just to clarify, I mean "Ahhh!" as in, "That really hurts!" Not "Ahhh," as in, "My, that's refreshing."

My second reaction was a profound feeling of empowerment. I feel as if my teeth finally respect me.

For years, I've been begging my teeth to straighten out. I've had numerous, lengthy conversations with them, imploring them to please, if it wouldn't be too much trouble, move over a tad and look pretty. I've warned them that if they didn't, something horrible would happen.

But I was wholly ignored. The reason? No respect. My teeth didn't think I'd get tough with them—that I'd back up my words.

But they were wrong. Way wrong. They pushed me too far and I went all oral surgeon on 'em.

Now that I've had eight teeth pulled, my remaining teeth have to believe that I mean business. From my teeth's perspective, I am the Mafia. To them, having one tooth pulled is the equivalent to a Mob hit. What I just did is a tooth massacre. They'll never rest easy again.

My conversations with my teeth these days have taken on more of a tough-guy tone. I look in the mirror and say things like, "I had those other teeth for thirty-five years and then just yanked 'em out. And I didn't shed one tear doing it, either. Do you think any of you are any more special to me than them?"

The mistake my teeth made was overestimating their value to me. Now that I'm living with three-fourths the number of teeth that I used to have, I realize that teeth are largely overrated. That means mine had better straighten up, and I mean now, or I'll pull every last one of them, and replace them with dentures. Let them just try me and see if I won't.

And I think word of my new tough-guy attitude is spreading to the rest of my body too. I've found that if I stare at my arm too long, it starts shaking nervously. It knows I'm not one to trifle with. If I took out some teeth, why not a limb?

We live in a world of medical marvels. Doctors can replace just about any part of your body now, and often the replacement works better than the original. This means the rest of my body better start behaving or I'm going totally bionic.

Yes, it might be that I'm being a wee bit harsh with my body. I'm certainly glad the Lord has more mercy than I do.

There was a time early in my Christian walk when I believed that God was scrutinizing every move I made, waiting for me to blow it. It took me a while to learn that "the steadfast love of the LORD never ceases, his mercies never come to an end" (Lamentations 3:22 RSV).

I know that God is very much aware of my failings, but I also know that he is ready to forgive me, no matter what I've done and no matter how far I've fallen.

So, in the spirit of mercy, instead of pulling the rest of my teeth, I've thrown them all in jail. They are literally behind teeny little bars in my mouth now, and they won't see the light of day for the next two years. After that, it's probation (wearing a retainer) for who knows how long. If it turns out they didn't learn their lesson, if they go astray again, then it's back in the slammer.

Or, who knows? Maybe I'll pull a few more of them, just to let 'em know who's boss.

part 5
Psychosomatic
(It's All in His Head)

chapter 18

Gall Bladder Surgery

Just to try something different, I thought I'd start off the new year by having my gall bladder removed. Just about bedtime on January 4, I started having severe upper-abdominal pain. After about an hour of enduring this pain, I finally surrendered and went to the emergency room, where I was forced to wait an additional three or four hours before being treated.

I'm not complaining about emergency room service, though, because I really do sympathize with the workers there. I feel it's only right that if you do happen to be experiencing something like massive congestive heart failure, the least you can do is call ahead and let the good folks at your local ER know you'll come in whenever it's convenient for them.

So, long story made short, I had the offending body part taken out. Apparently it's totally useless and you don't even need it. It's just like your tonsils, appendix, or a cosmetology degree. That there can be parts of your body that you don't even need is an amazing concept to me. It makes me wonder what else they're going to discover that we don't need in the future.

"Hey, y'know that heart-pumpy-thingy in your chest? Turns out you don't even need it! Make sure you hang onto those ear lobes, though. You don't want to lose those!"

So, I've been talking about this experience and I'm amazed at the number of people who tell me they also have had their gall bladder removed. It seems to be a rite of passage into middle age. It's like a secret society of geezers out there with missing body parts. I guess I've arrived.

It definitely wasn't the most pleasant way I could have rung in the new year, but my doctor told me it was necessary—that the gall bladder was in pretty bad shape. In order to keep the rest of my body healthy, the unhealthy part had to be removed.

It works the same way in our spiritual lives. In 2 Corinthians 13:5, Paul exhorts us to examine ourselves to see if we are in the faith. That means we have to take a hard look at our thoughts, actions, ambitions, and motives.

If we find anything out of conformity with God's will, do you know what we're to do? In Matthew 5:30, Jesus says, "If your right hand causes you to sin, cut it off." That's right. Have it surgically removed. Pretty tough language; but if something exists in our lives that is not pleasing to the Lord, it can poison the rest of our lives, just like a diseased gall bladder.

By the way, I wonder if the secret society of gall-bladderless old geezers has a secret handshake? I guess I'll be notified.

chapter 19

Med Depot

Hopefully, I will soon be the proud father of a brand new kidney stone. I found out I was "with stone" a couple weeks ago when the little fella announced his presence with the traditional blinding bout of pain. Ah, stones. What're you gonna do with 'em?

I'm hoping this one's a pioneer stone, the kind that wants to explore the great beyond and see what's out there, rather than a settler stone that thinks the spot he's in might be a good place to settle down and raise a family.

Running back and forth to the doctor's office these days gives me pause. Surely there must be some aspects of practicing medicine that we patients could do ourselves. Take, for example, guessing what's wrong with the patient and then telling him to come back in two weeks if the prescription doesn't work. We could pretty much handle that by ourselves without a doctor's assistance, couldn't we?

And this thought leads me to my next billion-dollar business idea. Feel free to use it. I've got plenty of others.

How about this: We have Home Depot helping us build it ourselves. We have Office Depot helping us run our own businesses. Why not have a Med Depot, where medical do-it-yourselfers can get supplies to do all those procedures that we would normally pay big bucks to have professionals do for us?

Of course, we'll still leave all the heavy lifting to the doctors. Those tricky procedures such as heart transplants, brain surgery, and robbing us blind, we'll continue to let the experts handle.

But I see wide-open opportunity in other areas, such as cosmetic surgery. Can it really be that hard? Take that part out. Tighten that up. Remove that. Personally, I think we're ready to try it.

I can hear the commercials now.

> "So, Carl, I'm going in Friday to get a hair transplant."
>
> "You're not going to pay someone to do that for you, are you, Frank?"
>
> "Well, sure. What else can I do?"
>
> "You ought to get on down to Med Depot. They've got Full-Growth Hair Transplant kits on sale this week for only $29.95!"
>
> "Really?"
>
> "Sure! And while you're there, why don't you pick up a LypoQuick System to take care of that unsightly truck inner tube you carry around your waist?"
>
> "Heh, heh. Yeah, I see what you mean, Carl! Thanks for the recommendation. You're a pal!"
>
> Announcer: "Folks, next time you need superfluous medical treatment, think Med Depot!"

Of course, some surgeries we just can't do without—such as the kind mentioned in Ezekiel 36:26: "I will give you a new heart and put a new spirit in you; I will remove from you your heart of stone and give you a heart of flesh."

The picture here is of an old heart that is beyond repair and in need of replacement. (Talk about getting some bad news at the doctor's office.) The good news, of course, is that even though there's no hope for the old heart, a transplant is possible and comes with a 100 percent chance of success. After all, it's God doing the operation, right?

It's amazing to me the extraordinary measures the Lord goes to in order to demonstrate his love for mankind. He'll do surgery and not even charge us for it. And I believe that's because he's already paid the price.

By the way, just a word to my good doctor buddies out there: Hi guys! You see how I kid all of you. I'm a joker, all right! Of course you know that I think all those involved in your noble and highly valued profession are very important. No need to get offended and blacklist me or anything. Ha, ha. I'm just a harmless comedian, remember? You know how silly we are! Well, now, no hard feelings, right? Okey-dokey then!

chapter 20

Kidney Punch

I recently discovered that I had a stone of the kidney variety, and in August I wound up having an outpatient procedure to have it removed.

We just received the hospital bill, which was around $12,000. Thank God we have insurance! Since that is the most expensive stone I've ever purchased, I thought it'd be a good idea to have it mounted on a ring for my wife. She, however, failed to see the romance in this gesture and was impervious to my most vehement arguments.

"Just imagine, honey. Other women are sitting around showing off their rubies, sapphires, and diamonds, and you flash a $12,000, eight-millimeter stone at 'em!" She didn't budge, so I guess I'll be wearing it.

Anyway, two operations for two different kinds of stones in one year is quite an achievement. Quite a painful achievement, but pain is a part of life.

Psalm 34:19 says, "A righteous man may have many troubles." There is no promise in the Bible that I know of that says we're going to get through life without any pain.

During 9/11, our country experienced tremendous pain. In response to the attack, we experienced an exponential increase in negative emotions such as grief, anger, and fear. Fear of war, fear of a failing economy, and fear of what those things meant to our families.

So how are we, as Christians, supposed to respond in times of national tragedy and crisis? It was amazing and uplifting to see people all over the country respond to the material needs of the victims of the attack, but what about the spiritual needs of the nation?

I heard that some churches adopted the position that people were much too distracted and depressed to be reached in that moment. But it seemed to me that as the pain increased, so did the need and opportunity for ministry.

It has been my experience that, now more than ever, people need to know that God hasn't gone anywhere. The rest of the Scripture I just quoted says, "but the LORD delivers him from them all." The world needs to know (and we Christians need to remember!) that "God is our refuge and strength, an ever-present help in trouble" (Psalm 46:1). God is still good, his arm is still strong, and he still delights in helping his children.

That knowledge alone should embolden us to take more risks in ministry—attempt the untried, jump out into the unknown, and dare to do something great for God. And if we fail? Then we fail marching forward in obedience to the Lord, rather than retreating to the mirage of comfort and safety.

And me? I plan to do my part by continuing to bring the healing balm of humor and encouragement to people all over the country. People were in desperate need of a respite from the heaviness that enshrouded our country after the attacks. It was my prayer then and continues to be now that after they experience the joy of the Lord for just a little while, they'll be strengthened to rise to the challenges that lie ahead.

So, look for me on the road. I'll be the one wearing the not-yet-fashionable kidney stone ring. Hey, it's a $12,000 ring!

chapter 21

Mom's Cold Remedies

I just caught a cold and feel really lousy. I don't think it detracts from my masculinity at all to say I want my mommy.

Okay, now that I see it in print, I admit it detracts from my masculinity.

But it's amazing how Mom always used to know exactly what to do when I got sick, and she invariably had a treatment plan that was even more dreadful than the illness itself.

At the first sign of the sniffles, Mom would produce one of those old glass thermometers that I had to hold in my mouth for so long that my chin would begin to quiver uncontrollably and my jaw felt like it was going to fall off.

If I had a fever that was anything less than life-threatening, then off to school I went. If the thermometer revealed I was indeed knocking on death's door—or, if not knocking at his door, then at least hanging around in his subdivision somewhere—Mom would proceed to the second stage of treatment, which involved administering a dose of rotgut whiskey, which is also known in some communities as "NyQuil."

They've since changed the formula, but back when I was growing up, NyQuil was about ninety proof and was so potent you could get tipsy by just walking past the medicine cabinet.

Interesting historical note: Archaeologist James R. NyQuil discovered his now-famous cold remedy in 1872 while excavating an ancient Native American archaeological site in southern Arizona. His team unearthed "a foul-smelling liquid" which was thought to be used as an embalming fluid.

Human nature being what it is, the entire archaeological team agreed they should all take a sip "and see what happens." The few that didn't suffer a sudden, horrific death were almost instantaneously cured of their colds. This draught eventually became a tremendous commercial success and remains to this day a popular cold remedy and paint remover.

After giving me medicine, Mom would shuttle me off to bed, slather about three inches of Vicks VapoRub all over my chest, and then button my pajama top over it. Nothing helps a kid drift off to sleep like having his jammies pasted to his body with a sticky, gelatinous substance that smells like axle grease.

I'm not sure what this action was supposed to accomplish, but Mom believed in Vicks VapoRub, just as if Moses had brought it with him down from Mt. Sinai or something. Any questions about its effectiveness were not to be broached and were immediately dismissed.

Finally, Mom would set up a nefarious contraption known as a humidifier, which continuously pumped thick clouds of vapor into my room. This served to distract me from my sticky jammies by transforming my bedroom climate into that of a primordial rain forest. All night long I would have terrible nightmares of being chased through the jungle by dinosaurs who caught me and spit axle grease all over my chest. It was awful.

When I awoke in the morning, I couldn't see more than three feet in front of me because of the thick cloud hanging in the air. The first time this happened, I thought that my cold had been a lot worse than originally thought and that I was now enveloped in heavenly clouds.

Fortunately for kids today, Mom's method of treating colds was outlawed in the mid-1980s and is now used only to interrogate terrorists.

But whatever strange methods Mom used to treat my colds, I never doubted her love for me. She always came to my rescue when I was hurting. I think one reason good parents are put on this earth is to paint a small picture of what God's personality is like. I believe that when we see something good in human nature, it is a reflection of God's personality. Because I have known my parents' love, it's easier for me to imagine my heavenly father caring for me when I'm hurting.

And now that I'm an adult and have kids of my own, I try to give them the very best care I can when they're sick. And by that, of course, I mean that I goof off and let their mom handle it.

part 6
Fitness Fixation

chapter 22

New Year's Health Plan

I 've been frustrated with the health advice from the so-called experts lately, because most of it is either far too difficult to follow or just flat-out wrong. It makes me think that even I could come up with a health plan that is just as good as theirs, if not better.

And so I have.

The following are my revolutionary new health tips to get you started on the right foot at the beginning of the year:

1. *Eat more grease.* I believe that scientists of the future will discover that grease, because it's a lubricant, actually helps your blood slide through your veins and arteries with greater ease. Therefore, the greasier the food, the better it is for you. I predict that one day paramedics will no longer perform CPR on heart attack victims, but will administer french fries and donuts instead.

2. *Exercise less.* The phrase "use it or lose it" is just way wrong. Have you ever noticed that everything on the planet wears out with more use? Why should the human body be any different?

   No, if you want to be really healthy, try to move as little as possible. Find a couch, get on it, don't move, and start improving your health today. The compliment of the future will sound something like, "Dude, you're a real couch potato!" or "Man, I've never seen anyone look so out of shape!"

This is one more reason we need to step up the robotics program in Japan. We're going to need plenty of household attendants to prepare our meals and carry us to bed after a hard day of lounging around watching M*A*S*H reruns.

3. *Gain weight.* I heard a story not long ago about an overweight grocery clerk who was shot in a hold up. Fortunately, the bullet was diverted by the clerk's multitudinous flab and he not only survived the attack, but wound up clobbering the would-be thief. A story like that has got to be true.

The point is, I think the guy might have something there. If all these organs we carry around are so important, doesn't it just make sense to take them out of harm's way by wearing as much padding around them as possible? The thicker the layer of flab you're sporting, the more of a bullet-deflecting, criminal-trouncing grocery clerk you'll be.

4. *Get more stress in your life.* Just as a little wind resistance makes a tree's roots grow stronger, stress will fortify and prolong your life. The reason we Americans have so many health problems is that we're living pampered, cushy, stress-free lives.

Take a look at the World War II generation. Those guys went straight from high school to battling Nazis. Now that's stress. Afterward, most of them went on to live to be about a gazillion years old. The secret of their longevity? One word, my friends: Stress, and plenty of it.

The first thing you need to do in order to get more

stress is have some kids. Having done that, then go fight some Nazis. If your kids are Nazis, you can rest assured you're stressing at maximum level. Now you can concentrate on staying as still as possible, eating greasy foods, and placing your order for a Japanese robot.

I know it's hard to filter through all the advice thrown at you these days. It seems everybody has an opinion and doesn't mind sharing it. The problem is knowing which advice to follow and which to mentally delete.

The only guaranteed method of ascertaining truth I've found is to seek the Lord. Proverbs 3:5–6 says, "Trust in the LORD with all your heart and lean not on your own understanding; in all your ways acknowledge him, and he will make your paths straight." I've learned that things will work out for the best if I prefer God's opinion over my own or anyone else's. And that applies to every area of my life, including my health.

As I review this chapter, though, I see now that my health plan relies far too heavily on robotic servants, and this, of course, is just foolishness. Sure, we'll need some robots, but we should not overlook developing a race of genetically enhanced supermonkeys as well.

chapter 23

Losing My Glubs

I t's now officially summertime. I know this because I'm feeling the primordial tug to lose weight. It's not that I'm trying to be more attractive, because I'm already married and therefore don't really have to look good anymore.

When I first received this revelation, I embarked upon a year-long pursuit of slovenly behavior and physical neglect that led me to the point where I am now—that of not being able to button my pants. Thus, I am implementing the following weight-loss regimen:

1. Cutting out every food that makes life interesting.
2. Doing something called "exercise," which I've come to learn is a fancy way of saying "manual labor."

Why is it that a guy will pay good money to have someone do his yard work for him and then turn around and fork over more cash for a health club membership?

Want a workout program? Here's an idea. Join Charles's Fitness Club! I have advanced exercise machines that you can push around my yard while benefiting from a thorough aerobic workout. Don't worry about buying any expensive workout togs either. Just wear some old, worn-out clothes like the kind you'd wear to, say, do yard work.

How much weight am I trying to lose? About one glub.

The word *glub* is derived from the Latin word *glubus*, which, when translated, literally means "disgusting roll of fat." It is that portion of your belly that you grab when you look in the mirror and say, "Sheesh, I need to lose weight."

If you need both hands to grab it, that's what you call two glubs. If you have your wife come in and grab the third glub, that's what you call a strange relationship that is in need of professional counseling.

Forget about pounds and inches. What we all want to lose is our glubs. Why not just say it?

Sometimes people scoff when I tell them I'm trying to lose weight, because they think I'm too skinny to have to worry about it. They believe this because I don't advertise my glubs. Glubs should never, and I mean never, be seen. They should be locked away like *The Idiot's Guide to Nuclear Bomb Construction.*

But I've noticed that glubs aren't the only thing we hide from each other, are they? In this country of "I'm fine. How're you?" we routinely mask our insecurities and weaknesses so that people will think the best of us.

The downside is if we never share the deep undercurrents of our lives, then our relationships are only ankle deep. Let's be honest. Everyone has difficult times in their relationships and finances. Everyone struggles with sin. Why can't we share these difficulties with each other?

In John 14:6, Jesus said, "I am the way and the truth and the life." It seems to me that truth does appear to be an integral part of the gospel, doesn't it? As Christians, we aren't called to present a facade of perfection to the world but to proclaim a God who is present and relative in a world of turmoil. In short, in order to communicate a real God, we might have to start getting real ourselves.

So how are my glub-reducing efforts going? Thus far, my

attempts have been typical, by which I mean I've gained about five or six pounds, or one-half glub.

Which reminds me—I am now accepting applications for my fitness club. I'll have your exercise equipment standing by.

chapter 24

Getting Fiscally Fit

There's no time like the present to get your finances in order and take the necessary measures to secure your financial future. In the interest of helping you accomplish this task, I offer a few of my own financial tips that have served me so well over the years.

1. *Organize your bills.* For most people, the subject of bills is unpleasant, but it needn't be anymore. Instead of ignoring them, I suggest you tackle financial responsibilities as I do by organizing your bills into three categories: Past Due, Way Past Due, and I'm Going to Have to Find Another Place to Live Next Month.

   Congratulations! Your bills are now organized!

   After completing this task, you will no doubt experience a deep sense of accomplishment. Feel free to reward yourself by using your credit card to buy lots of expensive stuff that you really don't need. You needn't worry about the bills for these purchases, because you now possess the financial expertise you need to handle them.

2. *Build a relationship with your banker.* This task will not be easily accomplished, because bankers are strange, reclusive creatures that should be approached with great care.

In the banking culture, even showing your face could greatly offend your banker, so when introducing yourself to him, wear some type of facial covering, such as a ski mask or nylon stocking.

You should also avoid verbally asking for money, as this is viewed as uncouth and crass. Instead, write your request down and hand it to your banker. Be sure to phrase your request boldly in as simple wording as possible. A phrase such as "Give me all your money" is ideal.

When you follow these suggestions, I think you'll find your banker will fall all over himself getting you the cash you requested, and you may safely assume your relationship with him is off to a great start.

3. *Learn to budget.* Creating a budget doesn't have to be difficult or restricting. Let's say you want to take an expensive vacation but it isn't in your budget. Does that mean you don't get to take the trip? Absolutely not!

Adding such an item to your budget is simple. Just take a piece of paper and write the word "Budget" at the top and just below it write the words "One expensive vacation."

Tah-dah! Now your dream vacation is in your budget! See how easy it is? Feel free to go ahead and call your travel agent right now.

4. *Learn to save money.* Saving money can be enjoyable and liberating. Suppose you have your eye on a nice, shiny BMW, but you know you should be saving money instead. How does one save money when buying a luxury car?

Try this. Go test-drive a Rolls Royce and decide to buy one. Next, come to your senses and realize you can't afford a Rolls and go buy the more moderately priced $50,000 BMW instead. Wow! You've just saved about a hundred grand.

Using this very same savings plan, my wife and I saved over $9 billion last year alone.

Does that make me a billionaire?

Yes, it does.

Financial worries definitely have a way of getting us down, don't they? One way to combat monetary distress is to educate yourself about money. And it's a good idea to get your input from someone who actually knows something about the subject, rather than from a comedian.

At the end of the day, though, there is no such thing as 100 percent security on this planet. In a world of chaos, anything can happen to destroy our financial castles. That's why, in addition to exercising good stewardship with our finances, we need to trust the Lord with the welfare of our families. "So do not worry, saying, 'What shall we eat?' or 'What shall we drink?' or 'What shall we wear?' . . . But seek first his kingdom and his righteousness, and all these things will be given to you as well" (Matthew 6:31, 33).

I don't think that's just some pretty verse that Jesus spouted off to make us feel better. I think it's a promise that you can take to the bank. Um, but you probably ought to leave your ski mask at home.

part 7

In-House Treatment

chapter 25

New House Purchase

My wife and I just realized a huge dream of ours by purchasing our very first home, located in Dacula, Georgia. Now let's get this out of the way right now. Dacula is pronounced Duh-CUE-la. Everybody always wants to rhyme it with Dracula or they pronounce it "Dah-cool-la." Wrong and wrong.

Anyway, moving was quite a change for us, because we had lived in our last apartment (which was really the basement of a split-level house, but it sounds better to say "apartment") for eleven years. The biggest adjustment we've had to make in our new house is that we can actually hear each other speaking now. For eleven years, our conversations were drowned out by the footsteps of our upstairs neighbors. Our conversations would go like, "Hey honey! I'm . . . THOOM STOMP STOMP . . . store. Do you . . . THOOM THOOM . . . anything for you?"

"Sure, . . . STOMP THOOM THOOM . . . on your way, okay?"

It had been years since I had heard my wife complete a sentence.

Another good piece of news is that we now have blankets to spare. It's been a dark, ugly secret of ours that we never got curtains for our back bedroom. Because we were renting and had no intention of staying there very long, we avoided the expense of curtains by draping our old blankets across the windows. Clever, huh? As a result, we never, and I mean never, allowed anyone in that back bedroom. We tried to play it cool, but every now and then one of our friends would wander back toward that bedroom and we'd both shriek, "DON'T GO IN THERE!" while diving in between them and the door. I'm sure they must've thought we had a body hidden back there.

I am also glad to report that our new house is much less dusty than our old one. That place was undoubtedly the dustiest place I've ever lived. It was incredible! You could completely dust and vacuum every square inch of the place and before you knew it, two or three years had passed and the place needed dusting again. Amazing!

In the foyer of our new house hangs a picture that I gave my wife on her last birthday, which was a couple of weeks after we signed the contract on our house. Because we had been so busy looking at houses, I was still shopping for her present a couple of days before her birthday. (Ah, who am I kidding? I waited that long to buy her present because I'm a guy, all right?!)

I had spent untold hours wandering aimlessly through racks of ladies clothing, studying dozens of pieces of jewelry, and perusing rows and rows of books. I had virtually exhausted all my usual resources and still had nothing for her. In addition to all that, I had gone through an extremely difficult situation earlier that day, and as a result, felt completely defeated. I was completely out of energy, ideas, and inspiration.

Finally, I remembered that my wife has an affinity for Thomas Kinkade pictures, so I wandered into his gallery in the mall. I was listlessly rummaging through the pictures when all of a sudden I found it. It was a picture portraying a turn-of-the-century family as they stand in front of their home, preparing to take a ride in their horse-drawn carriage. The lights are glowing in their quaint little cottage and you can almost feel the warmth emanating from this picturesque scene as it radiates peace, goodness, and simpler times.

But as wonderful as the picture was, I hadn't decided on buying it until I saw the verse attached to it—Joshua 24:15, "As for me and my household, we will serve the LORD." When I saw that verse, I was very still and felt a lump in my throat. All at once, all the defeats I had suffered that day came into focus and I could see them for what they were, and they didn't matter quite as much. At that moment, a new resolve stirred in my heart that seemed to say, "Come what may, good or bad, blessing or curse, I will follow Jesus."

We now have that very picture with that verse inscribed on it hanging in our foyer, reminding us of our purpose, resolve, and focus in our new home.

chapter 26

Remodeling My House

The big news in my life these days is that I bought an older house that I am remodeling. Yes, Virginia, comedians can do manual labor (although we don't like to advertise it).

It would be hard to chronicle in just one chapter all the repairs this house needs. It's been neglected for some time now and needs a lot of work. The good news is that I've been working on it and am getting a great deal of experience in the construction field.

Just the other day, while removing a cabinet in my half bath, I somehow managed to burst one of the pipes. In an instant, I went from Expert Home Renovator to Old Faithful Tour Guide. I remember standing there, dumbfounded, in the pouring rain (in a bathroom with no shower, mind you) thinking, "I probably should turn off the water main now." It's that type of crack decision-making that has placed me in the position of power I now enjoy. Through the experience, I learned that nothing says "welcome to your new home" like a pressurized water pipe exploding in your face.

To say the yard needs work is an understatement. Think dense, African jungle, add some pine trees, and you have the right picture. A friend of mine looked at my lawn/forest and wisecracked, "Who did your lawn?" Sensing a business opportunity, I answered, "I did. It's a design I like to call 'Primeval Rain Forest.' You want my card?"

People have disappeared into my yard, never to be heard from again. I'm not sure, but I think I might have some sort of tribe living back in there somewhere. Every now and then, I hear the sound of drums coming from the far corner of the back yard.

The whole project has taken a bit longer than I originally predicted. Based on the progress I've made so far, I am now able to project a finish date somewhere around the turn of this century—say about 2099 or so. It is my fond hope that my children and grandchildren will continue this noble effort.

As I work on this house, the one thing that keeps going through my mind is how much like my life it is. My life was a ruin with no hope at all—neglected, abandoned, and abused. Then, one day I awakened to the knowledge of God's love for me. He purchased me and is in the process of fixing me up. True, he's done a lot of work, but there is a lot more to be done. Like my house, long periods of time go by when it seems nothing is accomplished; but all the while, work is being done.

I sometimes think that the Lord led me to do this project to remind me of what he has done—and is doing—with me. And that's a comforting thought.

It's time for me to get back over to the house and start working again. If you don't ever hear from me again, please send a search and rescue party to my back yard. I think the natives might be getting restless.

part 8
Issues at Home

chapter 27
Birthing Faith

On Wednesday, February 13, 2002, my wife and I welcomed Faith Christina Marshall into the world as our firstborn.

When my wife told me that we were pregnant, my first comment was, "Praise the Lord!" My second comment was, "All right! New material!"

I immediately nicknamed my wife "Preggy Girl," much to her delight. When she started suffering memory loss due to a surging hormonal tide, I modified her nickname to "Preggy Brains." "Preggy Brains," however, was received much less favorably than the first version, so in a burst of inspired wisdom, I changed it back to "Preggy Girl."

In preparation for the delivery, we took all the usual classes, but when the moment of truth arrived, we promptly forgot every single thing we thought we had learned. You name it—what to do, when, and how—everything. My wife was two-thirds of the way through her labor before I remembered the breathing exercises.

So what were the classes for? The untold, secret purpose of the childbirth classes is for women to get even with men by luring in the naive, gullible, unsuspecting chumps (prospective dads), and then hitting them with every single bit of pregnancy reality they can stomach. In my class, several men didn't even make it through the Introduction of Terminology segment before bolting to the restroom.

Then they played THE VIDEO. They *love* to show THE VIDEO—a presentation of a real woman in real labor. Emphasis on real, as in *not the edited TV version*. By the time it ended, several men had passed out, while the rest of us sat there, white as sheets, trying to look like, "Yeah, I knew all that," while trying not to cry. All the while, the women weren't watching the video. No, they were watching the men, laughing their heads off, and thinking, "What a bunch of weenies!"

My least favorite part of the class, though, was learning the relaxation techniques they say every woman ought to know during pregnancy. Everyone grabbed a pillow and lay on the floor while whale music played over the sound system. All the while I was thinking, "I paid good money so that I could get up from my La-Z-Boy, miss my TV show, drive across town, find a parking space, lie on the floor with thirty other strangers, and listen to a bunch of sea life—so I could learn how to relax?" I got so stressed out thinking about it, that by the time I got out of there, I was mad at all sea life in general and whales in particular. I went home and ate three cans of tuna fish to register my protest and blow off some steam. I would have had whale steaks, but it seems you can't buy those anymore.

One of the really amazing things about our daughter's birth, though, is that she was born on her due date. How many kids are actually born on their due date? Three? Four? I even scheduled an event in Memphis on her due date because I thought, "What're the chances of her being born then?"

But at four o'clock that morning, my wife woke me up saying, "You're not going to Memphis today."

After a long, hard, wonderful, exhausting day of bringing our little one into the world, my wife insisted I go home to get some sleep. When I got home, I stumbled into the bedroom, fell into bed, and then remembered a little something I had forgotten to do. I got back out of bed and knelt down, but the words refused to come. Instead, the tears trickled down my cheeks, and then they flowed.

I remembered years of sacrifice and waiting. I remembered the many times I had asked the Lord to remember my wife's faithfulness, and all her sacrifice that made my ministry possible. I remembered telling my wife that the Lord wouldn't forget us. I remembered standing on the knowledge of God's goodness when it seemed there was no reason to believe anymore.

The Bible says in Psalm 37:4, "Delight yourself in the LORD and he will give you the desires of your heart." The Lord has proven himself in my life countless times, and he has done it once again through the miracle of the birth of our daughter.

I've heard people say that they've never heard God speak and have never seen any evidence of his existence. I've found he will make himself known to those who are willing to take a step of faith.

chapter 28

About to Have a Second Baby

It was only two short years ago that I was awakened by my wife at 4:00 AM and told it was time to go to the hospital. Now we're rapidly approaching that time again. Any day now, my wife will be delivering our second child, and the excitement is building in the Marshall household.

I really don't remember much at all about the first delivery. I remember there was a lot of high-pitched screaming, some fainting, and a bit of nausea. But, fortunately, the nurse came in, gave me a sedative, and I calmed down.

But seriously, I do remember thinking how unfair the whole process seemed. When they administered the epidural to my wife, they didn't offer me anything for my discomfort at all. In fact, the whole process seemed decidedly slanted in my wife's favor.

"Would you like an extra pillow, Mrs. Marshall?"

"How about some more ice, Mrs. Marshall?"

It just seemed unfair.

I pointed these things out to my wife a few days ago, but she seemed neither convinced nor amused.

The biggest surprise we received during the labor process was being told to take a nap after the epidural was administered. The nurse came in, dimmed the lights, and essentially told us to "take five." That's something they don't tell you about when you're taking all those Preparation for

Parenting classes. I guess they wouldn't register as many students if the whole spiel was, "Okay, you're probably not going to need any of this stuff, because you'll most likely be asleep."

I didn't remember any of the helpful tips that I learned in class anyway. During labor and delivery, my mind was more blank than an Arctic winter landscape. Two weeks after my daughter was born, when we were all at home with the baby, I finally remembered. "Oh yeah, honey. Remember to breathe!" She's lucky to have me.

It seems we go into so much of life unprepared. Everybody likes a perfect score, but it's impossible to do it all right the first time. When we experience difficulty or trials, it's important to remember a couple of things.

Number one, God is on our side and desires us to pass. Second, his grace is sufficient to see us through our greatest difficulty. No challenge is too great for God. No trial intimidates him. He never says, "Man, I never saw *that* coming! What are we gonna do?"

As I learn more about God, there are two indisputable facts I keep returning to:

1. God is good.
2. Jesus loves me.

When faced with life's most challenging obstacles, these are the truths that give me the greatest comfort. May God's grace be with you.

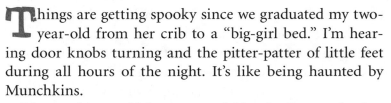

chapter 29
Nocturnal Wanderings

Things are getting spooky since we graduated my two-year-old from her crib to a "big-girl bed." I'm hearing door knobs turning and the pitter-patter of little feet during all hours of the night. It's like being haunted by Munchkins.

I knew this would happen, and it's why I argued vehemently to keep my daughter in her crib until her late teens. Unfortunately, my wife wouldn't have any part of it, and now I'm trying to creatively solve the problem of my little one's nocturnal wanderings.

Well, let me clarify. I'm a night person (I'm writing this around 1:00 AM), so any time before seven in the morning is nocturnal to me.

But this whole experience with my daughter's newfound freedom and the resulting sleep loss prompts the question, "Why hasn't anyone invented Velcro pajamas with the corresponding Velcro bed?" Of course, if you had the Velcro jammies, you wouldn't even need the bed. You could just stick the kids to a piece of felt on the wall and come back and get them in the morning. What a great idea! All those interested should contact me immediately to get in on this ground-floor opportunity.

I know what you're thinking: They've already invented a product to handle this situation. It's called duct tape. Yes, but I must tell you that I'm just a teensy bit hesitant to go that direction. Maybe when they come up with a Child Protective Services–friendly duct tape, I'll consider it. Until then, I'm a warden corralling a truant escapee back to bed.

It's my job. I'm the dad. It's dad's job to make sure everyone is tucked into bed. It's his job to make sure all the doors are locked and everyone's safe.

Sometimes I think about my heavenly father watching over me after I go to bed. The Bible says, "For he will command his angels concerning you to guard you in all your ways" (Psalm 91:11). Isn't it a comforting thought to think of God that way?

Yes, I know he's the all-powerful Creator and Lord, but he's also a father who watches over his children. He's a God who's big enough to create the universe but still loving enough to care for his children.

chapter 30

The Summer of the Bunnies

The summer of 2007 will forever be known in the Marshall household as "The Summer of the Bunnies."

On a steaming hot day in early July, I was laying sod in my back yard in the blistering sun. My vision was blurry and I felt like I was about to pass out as I wrestled the heavy squares of sod into position. (Okay, it was really only about eighty-five degrees that day, I'd only been working for about twenty minutes, and the sod was almost completely dried out. My toddler daughter could've easily carried it. But I'm laying the foundation for my defense of what is about to follow, so we'll just stick with the first version, okay?)

As I maneuvered yet another gargantuan square of sod into place, I heard a faint, bird-like screech emanating from somewhere in my immediate vicinity. I gave a cursory glance around the area but couldn't locate the source. After a few moments, I resumed my work only to hear the tiny cry again. This time, I identified the source immediately. The sound was emanating from beneath my foot. I had accidentally unearthed—and, even worse, stepped on—a nest of newborn bunnies. (Remember, I was almost senseless with heat fatigue, and therefore not at all responsible for my actions.)

In an almost panicked state, I knelt to examine the nest. Could I have inadvertently killed some baby bunnies? The

thought was simply unbearable. I would hate to kill anything so small, defenseless, and adorable, and it's the type of
thing you just don't want on your résumé: "July 2007: Killed
some baby bunnies."

I instinctively knew that kind of thing wasn't going to
help my career.

"We'd love to have you speak at our next function, Mr.
Marshall. Oh, wait a minute. What's this? Bunny killer?
We'll get back to you."

I did what I could to reconstruct the bunny nest, while
doing my best to keep from touching either the bunnies or
their home. I knew their mother would be hesitant to return to the nest if it smelled like humans.

Over the next two weeks, my family cautiously studied
the nest and marked the growth of the bunnies. Our prin-
ciple concern was whether the mother would abandon the
nest because of my interference. Fortunately, the bunnies
continued to grow at an exponential rate, and one day the
nest was empty. Mission accomplished, and my résumé remains unsullied.

Now the temperature is dropping outside, the leaves
are beginning to fall, and a new season is on the way.
Occasionally, I catch glimpses of young bunnies hopping
around my back yard, and I'm truly thankful they made it.

All of our lives are constructed of a multitude of such
dramas as we negotiate our way through the various seasons of life—sometimes through seasons of abundance and
rejoicing; sometimes through need and desire.

During the change of seasons in our lives, it is important
to realize that the Lord is ultimately in control. Daniel 2:21
says, "He changes times and seasons; he sets up kings and
deposes them. He gives wisdom to the wise and knowledge
to the discerning."

That means that, in all things, both great and small, God is in charge. He is aware of our plight and desires to assist us. He's big enough to know when a sparrow falls or even when a bunny is in trouble. And he's big enough to care for all his children.

chapter 31

The Black Hole

There is a place in my home that strikes terror in the hearts of all its inhabitants (all those over three feet tall, that is). It is a place that we try not to think about and that we avoid at all costs. The very mention of its name makes my wife and me shudder in revulsion and fear.

It's called the Black Hole.

The Black Hole is the default repository of all those sundry pieces of paper that we know we should probably keep but are too lazy to file. In our house, it's the bottom dresser drawer.

My wife used to be the organized person in our relationship. I am the sloppy one, or so she claims. My perspective is that I have a sophisticated organizational system which consists of tiny piles of paper strategically placed all over our house. If anyone (my wife) disturbs one of these piles in the guise of "cleaning up," it disrupts a delicate balance and results in a catastrophic outcome (i.e., I throw a temper tantrum).

My proof that my system works is that I can find any receipt, note card, or Post-It note almost instantly, which means I typically stumble across what I'm looking for after a couple days.

So, after the children came along, my wife had other things to keep up with (two baby "other things"), and therefore, incrementally, became more sloppy. She sees this as a deep personal failure akin to Anakin Skywalker being seduced by the dark side of the Force. I try to cheer her up by humming the Darth Vader theme song whenever she walks into the room, but I don't think it's working. I'd hate to think what she'd do to me if she were packing a light saber.

Terrifying as they may be, black holes are nothing to be ashamed of. In fact, every organism or organization on the planet has some type of black hole. On television, they keep all the stuff they don't want cluttering up the good channels in a place called the FOX network.

In our government, the black hole is called "Congress," and that's where we keep all the undesirable stuff we don't really need but at the same time are hesitant to throw away, such as politicians.

The weird thing is that we can even find black holes within ourselves. Everyone has a plethora of embarrassing things about themselves tucked away somewhere inside that they hope no one will ever see.

The Bible says, "O LORD, you have searched me and you know me" (Psalm 139:1). The thing is, God sees everything inside us, and still loves us, in spite of all the mess.

The good news regarding the Black Hole at my house is that I've finally found a solution. I boxed up all the stuff in the Black Hole and put it in the attic. The bad news is that, since then, my wife has started a brand new Black Hole. I think I'm going to need a bigger attic.

part 9

Excessive Food Swings

chapter 32

Starbucks Ice Cream Latte Loss

The only reason I'm writing this is to get my wife off my back. Also because she might have a point. And because I love this particular subject matter as much as she does. And because I have nothing else to do.

Maybe I should start at the beginning. Just after dinner one evening, my wife, in a move not terribly unlike Eve's in the Garden of Eden, slipped up behind me and told me to open my mouth and close my eyes. Because she's usually pretty trustworthy, I complied. What followed was a taste sensation I had hitherto not experienced. The origin of this delectable delight was Starbucks White Chocolate Latte ice cream.

There are certain moments you remember in life—your first kiss, your wedding day, the birth of your children, and your first taste of Starbucks White Chocolate Latte ice cream. The moment it touched my tongue, I was instantly transported to a happy place where all things are wonderful and time has no meaning. For me, it was kind of like being at Home Depot.

You've heard of some foods being sinfully good? If this particular ice cream had been around back in Moses' day, there would have been eleven commandments instead of ten. I mean it.

Who knows? There may even be some untranslatable

phrase in one of the Dead Sea Scrolls, placed just after the Ten Commandments that goes, "Oh, and one more thing, Moses. Tell everyone to stay away from that Starbucks White Chocolate Latte ice cream. Ooowee, is that stuff good!"

All right. Now that I have you all jazzed about the ice cream, I'll break the bad news to you.

They don't make it anymore. That's right. My wife e-mailed Starbucks and confirmed it. They have discontinued the flavor.

It's okay. Let it out. Remember, crying is a vital part of the mourning process.

The elimination of this product makes perfect sense to me, though, because everything my wife and I go ga-ga for either goes out of business, is taken off the market, is outlawed, or all of the above. Start praying now that we don't discover your favorite foods, restaurants, and toiletry products.

So, my wife, believer in me that she is, thinks that if I write about this subject, it will serve as a catalyst for a national, groundswell movement to bring back our favorite ice cream. I think she envisions Starbucks being bombarded with thousands of e-mails and phone calls requesting— no, make that, demanding—that this wonderful flavor be once again placed into production. She sees Jesse Jackson, Pat Robertson, and possibly even former child star Gary Coleman (if he's not already booked) leading a million-man march in front of the Starbucks headquarters in Seattle.

Such is my wife's vision. Such is her resolve. Such is her ice cream addiction. She will not be gainsaid in this matter. She will not be moved. (Translation: I'm going to keep hearing about this unless I give in and write the silly chapter.)

So, if this insane little gambit actually works and Starbucks starts making the flavor again, you'll have to taste-test it and tell me if you agree.

And speaking of taste-testing, Psalm 34:8 says, "Taste and see that the LORD is good." (Clever transition, huh?)

That's how confident God is. Once you experience an authentic relationship with him, you'll find that he can be trusted with all the things that matter most in your life—your hopes, your fears, your relationships, your finances, everything.

Engaging in a relationship with Jesus is not a laborious, eat-your-spinach experience. It's much more . . . well, delicious, like diving into a bowl of your favorite ice cream, with no weight-gain repercussions or consequences.

And one of the best things about this particular source of goodness is that the Lord will never be discontinued, unlike a particular ice cream flavor I may have mentioned elsewhere in this chapter.

Oh, and about the ice cream—I should mention that the White Chocolate Latte flavor is slightly addictive, but don't let that keep you from joining my cause. Just think about all the health-care workers that are out of work at the Starbucks Detox and Rehab Centers. Those people need jobs too.

part 10
Holiday Blues

chapter 33

A Man's Approach to Valentine's Day

I don't know why I always wait until the last minute to buy my wife's Valentine's Day present. Most likely, it's because I'm a guy.

It's a terrifying ordeal trying to pick out a Valentine's Day card on Valentine's Day evening, because there is absolutely no selection left. I don't know who else could have bought up all the good cards, because all the men on the planet are standing right there beside me in the greeting card aisle.

The only cards left by that time are written in some strange, soap opera–type language that I don't even understand. They say things like, "My Darling, blah-blah rose petals something something cherish you yada yada eternity."

Let me tell you, I'm as romantic as the next guy, but if I go home with a card like that, my wife is going to look at me like I just beamed down from the planet Weirdonia.

But the same thing happens every year. About one week before Valentine's Day, I think that the big day is nowhere on the radar, so I figure I still have pul-lenty of time to shop for my wife. I decide to wait a bit longer and then I'll get right on it. Yesiree, I'm going to get right on it.

About one day before Valentine's Day, I realize it's time to start thinking about what gift to buy, so I decide to research the subject by watching lots of television.

Around 5:00 PM on Valentine's Day, I sense faint warning

bells deep within me. I begin to feel there is some impending danger that threatens not only my happiness but perhaps my life as well. I'm not sure exactly what it is. Maybe something to do with my wife—

At 5:02, I experience a foxhole-grade terror as I perceive what that little item is that has escaped my attention. It is only then that I begin my five-step Valentine's Day shopping ritual:

1. Go to the flower store and discover there are no flowers left. Get back in car and throw a mini temper tantrum.

2. Go to the candy store and discover there is a world chocolate shortage. Briefly contemplate purchasing my wife a pack of Skittles for Valentine's Day. Briefly contemplate an early death. Decide against the Skittles.

3. Rush to mall and enter swanky department store. Walk by the ladies' unmentionables department and turn beet-red. Kill thirty minutes trying to work up enough nerve to enter said department. Enter ladies' unmentionables department and get ugly looks from every woman within visual range. Have a moment of stark clarity, becoming aware that I never was, and never will be, the type of guy who can shop for that kind of stuff. Tear out of ladies' unmentionables department like a convict with a pack of bloodhounds at his heels.

4. Enter regular women's clothing department and become aware I have no idea what size my wife wears. Experience momentary elation as I remember her measurements are 48-38-7, but then realize that is

my bicycle lock combination, not my wife's measurements. Plummet into deep depression.

5. Resign myself to buying my way out of the dilemma. Go to jewelry store and wait in line behind about fifty thousand other schmoes who are in the same predicament as I am.

It's a shame that Valentine's Day can turn into one more thing on our list to accomplish, isn't it? That doesn't seem like a very good way to celebrate our relationships.

Sometimes, our relationship with God can be that way. We can go through all the motions without experiencing a real connection with our loving father. All of the trappings of Christianity—church services, reading the Bible, praying, etc.—can either be opportunities to connect with God, or just more stuff to tick off our lists in an effort to make sure we don't get in trouble. If the latter is our motive, then we've managed to miss the romance of knowing God.

Speaking of romance, I have decided that this year is going to be different. I plan to go ahead and get a jump on shopping for a gift for my wife, right after I watch a little tele— . . . um, do some Valentine's Day gift research.

chapter 34

The Choices of Thanksgiving

Thanksgiving is almost here, and I'm all atwitter with anticipation. In celebration, I plan to once again partake in the age-old tradition of gorging myself with an embarrassing amount of food, creating gastrointestinal problems the like of which are rarely experienced in industrialized countries.

This year my family and I are planning to eat out on Thanksgiving Day, and we're in serious discussion regarding the restaurant.

Restaurant selection is a big decision that you don't want to botch. The main issue, as I see it, is whether you want to be waited on or would rather serve yourself at a buffet.

If you choose to be served, then your greatest challenge, of course, will be your waiter. Waiters are a strange and mysterious group of people who have their own language and moral code, not unlike the ancient Druids or the David Hasselhoff Fan Club. Those attempting to interact with them must be aware that their language and ours do not necessarily mean the same things.

For example, when the waiter gestures toward your empty plate and says, "Can I get that out of the way for you?" he really means, "It's time for you to go now."

When a waiter places your check on your table and says,

"Can I get anything else for you?" he really means, "It's time for you to go now, but leave your credit card."

When a waiter serves your food in a timely manner with a smile on his face, it means he did something gross to your entrée back in the kitchen.

Eating at a restaurant with a wait staff has other drawbacks too, like being served by an overworked waiter who would just as soon see you choke on a roll as have you ask for another glass of tea. Because they're desperately trying to avoid having one more thing to do, these waiters often wait until your mouth is packed like a chipmunk's before asking if you need anything else.

There's no way to win in this situation. Your best alternative is to attempt the complicated motor activity of chewing while shaking your head "no." You'll most likely wind up looking like a bobble-head doll, but that's infinitely better than the alternative, which is holding up your empty tea glass and saying something like, "May ah pweeb haf pum more pea?"

Personally, I would prefer to eat at a buffet, providing the following conditions can be accommodated:

A. I can get permission to scoot my chair up to the buffet and eat right there, instead of having to be bothered with all those pesky trips back and forth to and from my table, and

B. There is some type of national standard (or law, if you will) to dictate behavior in the buffet line—namely, just choose a food type, put it on your plate, and move on already. I always get stuck in line behind the guy who weighs each food selection as if he's making an important life decision.

It's a buffet! You're not buying a house. You're not

having surgery. If you make the wrong choice, just come back and get something else! This is America, by jingo, and that's how we do things here.

Of course, one of the most difficult parts of Thanksgiving is the subtle pressure of knowing that sometime during the day you're expected to muster up a little thankfulness. And where does this thing called "thankfulness" come from, anyway?

I have found that, just like my TV remote control, thankfulness is easiest to find when I'm not looking for it. It seems that when I concentrate instead on the good things God has placed in my life—my family, my ministry, my Rolls Royce (kidding!)—thankfulness comes easily.

The Bible says, "Blessed are the pure in heart, for they will see God" (Matthew 5:8).

I believe God's hand may most easily be seen in the countless graces we experience throughout each day. When we learn to recognize the author of these good things that have been placed in our lives, thankfulness is a natural by-product.

So, when you're home nibbling on your third helping of turkey and sweet potato pie, think of me at the restaurant, and pray that the waiter hasn't done anything gross to my food.

chapter 35

The Santa Recall Vote

I was five years old when I found a tiny baby doll in my Christmas stocking. To make matters worse, Santa had given my sister a toy fire truck that I intuitively knew should've been mine. It took years of therapy to get over the trauma.

How could Santa make such a colossal blunder? What else might he be messing up? Was he just flying around, dispensing toys higgly-piggly in heaven-only-knows whose stockings? A kid in Zambia gets an ice fishing kit? An Eskimo child gets an elephant saddle?

My confidence further eroded as I examined Santa's historical records, otherwise known as Christmas songs. For example, "Rudolph, the Red-Nosed Reindeer" states: "Then one foggy Christmas Eve . . ."

That's foggy, mind you. Not snowy. Not blizzardy. Just foggy.

". . . Santa came to say, 'Rudolph with your nose so bright, won't you guide my sleigh tonight?'"

I find it astounding that Santa—this amazing problem-solver, who routinely crams toys for all the children of the entire earth into one sleigh and then delivers them in one night, and has even figured out a way to make reindeer fly—is stumped by fog. Let a little mist roll in and he's completely dumbfounded.

"Uh-oh. Looks like we've got fog. Never seen this before.

Unless I can find a mammal with some sort of luminescent appendage, we're gonna have to call the whole thing off."

What about a couple of fog lights, Santa? Shouldn't the song be: "I got me a couple o' halogens, now I can make my rounds again!"

To me, it sounds like Santa is just looking for a reason to goof off. Could the reason for his sloppy work of late be that he's ready to retire? It makes me wonder whether Santa is still fit for the job. Maybe it's time to start a Santa recall petition.

But that, of course, demands the question: Who could we get to fill the position?

The obvious replacement would be Arnold Schwarzenegger. The extra exposure could really benefit him as he advances toward his ultimate goal of controlling the universe.

My recommendation is that we let Santa stay on with the company, but transfer him to the Easter Egg Delivery Division. We could then promote the Easter Bunny to Santa's present job, so long as he promises not to needle Santa about it.

The best thing about Christmas, though, is also the most dependable—Jesus. In a world of uncertainty, it helps to know that there is a love that is willing to suffer any hardship for my benefit.

I've found that love to be the one constant on this planet, and I see it demonstrated nowhere more clearly than in God's sending his Son on a dangerous rescue mission to save mankind from an eternity spent apart from him.

By the way, regarding the Easter Bunny's promotion, we'll have to be sure that everyone keeps their dogs locked up on Christmas Eve. It wouldn't do for the kids to find Santa Bunny lying in front of the tree on Christmas morning. There isn't enough therapy in the world to treat that kind of trauma.

chapter 36

Christmas Trials

When I was growing up, the thing that we looked forward to every Christmas morning was discovering what treasures our Christmas stockings held. Looking back, though, it was always a little disappointing. From the calf down to the ankle, I could count on my stocking being filled with mixed nuts and a softball-size clump of melted hard candy that Santa most likely picked up in a bargain bin at Kmart the preceding January.

From the ankle down to the toe, I would inevitably find an apple, orange, and tangerine, in that order. I always thought that was sort of odd and wondered why I got fruit for Christmas. Was it the money? C'mon, Santa. A bag of Snickers bars takes about the same amount of space and doesn't cost that much more. Just buy one and dump it in!

When I asked my mom why I was getting fruit for Christmas, she told me that Santa wanted me to eat more healthily. That seemed particularly hypocritical to me as I envisioned Santa's rotund frame in comparison to my Third World physique. It just didn't seem fair that I was leaving him milk and cookies and he was leaving me produce.

As an adult, Christmas can be pretty hard too. It's the one time of year when you are forced to spend time with people that you would ordinarily cross the street to avoid. Have you ever noticed that your tongue is sore after the holidays?

It's from biting it while your relatives are visiting. If your tongue is not hurting on New Year's Day, then it's a good bet your relatives are ticked off at you.

One of my favorite things about Christmas is connecting with my children. I love watching them as they experience the decorations, gift giving, and festivities for the first time in their lives. As they get older, I want to communicate to them that it is this very connection—a father's desire to commune with his children—that brought about the very first Christmas. It was a parent's passion for a lost child that drove God to interject himself into a hopeless world and caused him to reach through eternity to wrest his children from danger. Can you imagine such a God? I believe that type of love lies at his very heart and defines the deepest meaning of Christmas.

May you and your loved ones experience God's love this Christmas.

chapter 37

My Christmas History

C hristmas has often been a somewhat painful season for me. I grew up in a big household with five kids, so my parents were trying to cut corners any way they could. They would wait until about three days before Christmas to buy our Christmas tree, which was always a Scotch pine, the cheapest Christmas tree available on the entire planet. The Scotch pine normally retails for about $10 if you buy it a month before Christmas. Three days before Christmas, they are drier than a British sitcom, and the vendors will pay you to take them off their hands.

My parents would bring the tree home for my siblings and me to decorate. It was like having a six-foot cactus in our living room. I grew up thinking that emergency room visits were a normal part of the Christmas tree decorating experience. I usually lost about two pints of blood during the holiday season.

This year, the pain was of a different sort. My loving wife got me a radio-controlled airplane that I had been coveting—um, make that "praying for"—for quite some time. Unfortunately, I managed to land it in a tree on its fifth or sixth flight. I spent the next three and a half hours trying to rescue my plane, but was forced to give up when it started turning dark outside.

I must admit to thinking some rather un-Christmas-like

thoughts after about the second hour of the rescue mission. You have to understand; this was the second plane I had received for Christmas in my life. The first one I had gotten when I was about eleven years old, and I had managed to lose it on its maiden voyage as well. This may just be a guy thing, but I can't tell you how the thought of losing another Christmas plane galled me.

When I got home, I wasn't in the best of moods. After I calmed down a bit, I played with my daughter and just hung out with my wife. I even stopped swearing vengeance on that pine tree. I finally stopped feeling sorry for myself and remembered that the real blessings of God can't get stuck in trees. "But store up for yourselves treasures in heaven, where moth and rust do not destroy, and where thieves do not break in and steal. For where your treasure is, there your heart will be also" (Matthew 6:20–21).

I remembered that God has blessed me with a wonderful and healthy family. I also remembered the origin of Christmas, and that God was the one who gave the very first Christmas present. Sometimes it takes losing something to help us value the truly valuable things we have.

Fortunately, I didn't end up losing the plane. I returned the next day and had it out of the tree in about thirty minutes. I'd like to say I am completely over my Christmas day ordeal, but I must admit that sometimes I still find myself entertaining thoughts that involve a chain saw and a certain troublesome pine tree in Dacula, Georgia.

part 11
Criminally Inane

chapter 38

Hometown Interrogation

On a recent trip to the small town where I grew up, I decided to visit the old homestead. It had been years since I had seen the house where I was raised and predictably, everything looked much smaller.

As I wandered up the street, I paused and snapped a few pictures of my old neighborhood. Not long after I began my trip up memory lane, a police car pulled up beside me. An officer, who looked like he was about fourteen years old, questioned me thoroughly. Who was I? What was I doing there? Why was I taking pictures?

The policeman interrogated me for about ten minutes before reluctantly deciding I wasn't dangerous. He informed me there is a heightened awareness of suspicious activity in my old hometown since the 9/11 attacks.

Yes, that makes sense, I conceded. I could see all the terrorists plotting now.

"Okay, first we hit the World Trade Center, then the Pentagon. After that, we strike at the very heart of freedom and democracy by destroying Charles Marshall's old house." (Add appropriate accent when reading.)

It does seem that people are more guarded these days. Vigilance is a great idea, but the accompanying fear is one of the more disappointing products of 9/11. I can't help but notice that people are also experiencing fear over an uncertain economy.

This almost imperceptible veil of fear is especially disappointing when seen in the church. Aren't we the ones who are supposed to be leading the charge? Instead, I hear many pulling back, even from evangelical and outreach efforts, fearing the risk might be too great.

But I believe there is no better time to move forward than the present, especially in the cause of Christ. Joshua 1:9 says, "Have I not commanded you? Be strong and courageous. Do not be terrified; do not be discouraged, for the LORD your God will be with you wherever you go."

As Christians, we should be asking ourselves what hill needs charging. We should be asking where we can sign up for the all-or-nothing mission to take the message of Christ to the world.

Today, try asking yourself what you would do for Jesus if you had no fear. The answer might surprise you.

chapter 39

Stuck Behind the Prison Bus of Life

It seems like it's every other day that I get stuck behind a bus of some sort. Most of the time, it's a school bus that has to make about fifty stops between the front of my neighborhood and my house. Why hasn't anyone invented a bus with a bypass ramp that allows irate motorists to keep going right over the top of it?

The other day I was driving through my neighborhood and got stuck behind one of those prison work-detail buses. You know, the ones carrying the convicts who pick up trash on the side of the road?

Now, there's a concept that only government could embrace. Not that this is a bad idea, provided it takes place on the side of a highway somewhere, but we're talking about convicted criminals leisurely picking up trash right next to my neighborhood.

What do you suppose these guys have been locked up for anyway? Nothing too serious, I'm sure. Probably just acts such as burglary, breaking and entering, grand theft, and so forth. But for some reason, somebody thought it'd be a good idea to put these guys on a bus, presumably so as to acquaint them with areas of town they might not already be familiar with, such as my neighborhood.

This, of course, is a superb situation for the prisoners, because it allows them to case out my home while on the government clock. It's kind of like a work-study program for ambitious, career-minded criminals. This way, when they get out of prison, they'll be assured of a steady job (i.e., robbing my house and every other house in the neighborhood).

I don't know what else they could do to make it any easier for these guys to burgle my home, other than providing them with a tour guide on the bus to point out some of the more lucrative opportunities.

"Now coming up on your right, we have homes starting in the mid-150s with easy access and low security. Please make a note of 132 Elm on your left, which contains many valuable items such as televisions, DVDs, and stereos, all of which, may I remind you, are easy to pawn and hard to trace. Moving on . . ."

Not that I verbalize any of these sentiments while I'm waiting behind the prison bus.

I do hate waiting, though, and I particularly hate getting left behind. Have you ever gotten left behind in your life? Have you ever noticed a time when it seemed everyone around you was moving ahead, seeing their dreams fulfilled, while you were stuck behind the prison bus of life?

That's a tough place to find yourself. I know. I've run into the back of that bus so many times you can almost make out the license plate numbers imprinted on my forehead.

The good news lies in the fact that God's got it under control. Psalm 31:14–15 says: "But I trust in you, O LORD; I say, 'You are my God.' My times are in your hands."

To me, that means that even though it seems I've stalled out on the freeway of life, there is another way of viewing my situation. It might well be that, instead of God preventing me from advancing, he might well be preparing me for the road ahead. It might just be that, instead of keeping me from the things I want, the Lord is keeping me safe from those things that might harm me.

The one constant in this world is God's love, and that's true whether you're the one picking up trash on the side of the road or the one sitting in your car waiting.

Oh, by the way, remind me to check my home insurance policy. It never hurts to make sure those things are up-to-date.

chapter 40

My Argument
for Master
Criminal Status

I was at the store the other day, writing a check for $2.47, when the cashier asked for my identification. I was deeply offended at this request, not because it implied I might be a criminal, but because it implied I might be a petty criminal.

I don't think I'm just flattering myself when I say I believe I'm worthy of being mistaken for a master criminal like Doctor Doom or Magneto or even Wile E. Coyote.

I don't even come close to matching the petty criminal profile that I've observed on *COPS*, which, as everyone knows, is well known for its complete absence of master criminals. Based on this show, I offer two reasons why I feel I'm above petty criminal suspicion.

1. I wear shirts. The suspects on *COPS* are rarely ever seen wearing shirts. It seems to me that if the authorities were serious about stopping crime, a good place to start would be making sure everyone wears shirts. There seems to be something about going around half-naked that makes folks want to take drugs and pass bad checks.

    The general rule of thumb is, the more clothing

a person is wearing, the less crime they're likely to commit. I reference the Eskimos as proof. I challenge anyone to find footage of an Eskimo leaning against his dog sled getting patted down by a cop. It just doesn't happen.

In contrast, what do you observe when you look at old Tarzan films? You see a guy running around the jungle in a loincloth, pestering all the animals and getting into everybody's business. Yep, that Tarzan was trouble all right. If someone had slapped an Armani suit on him, the jungle would have been a better place for it.

The old saying, "clothes make the man," ought to be amended to "clothes make the man law-abiding."

2. I have no piercings or tattoos. I'm not saying that everyone who has a piercing or tattoo is a criminal. What I am saying is that just about every petty criminal I've ever seen is covered with them.

This is one of the very things that makes the petty criminal a petty criminal—the inability to realize that having a large, easily recognizable tattoo on his shirtless chest is going to make him easier to identify and capture.

Running around shirtless, pierced, and tattooed is simply not the behavior of a master criminal. I have it on good authority that the Green Goblin would not have tolerated this kind of cheap posturing in his organization. And you certainly wouldn't want to be around Lex Luthor wearing your nose ring and sporting a "Lynyrd Skynyrd Lives!" tattoo.

If you do happen to see a shirtless, tattooed goon standing at your front door, here are some things you need to know:

1. He's not there to sell you financial planning and mutual funds.
2. He's not a Mormon trying to convert you.
3. He may very well be your daughter's prom date.

So, I'm watching *COPS* a few nights ago and I realize that there's a part of me that is tempted to believe that I'm better than those folks—that because I'm sitting in my climate-controlled home in my comfy chair, with my shirt on, I'm somehow above the behavior exhibited by the suspects shown on this television show.

And then it hits me that God loves every one of those people every bit as much as he loves me. I realize that not an episode airs that he doesn't grieve for his kids on that program and long for their rescue. And if I were to be honest with myself, I know that I could have been on the same path, were it not for God's saving grace.

So, maybe the next time I get carded for writing a check, I don't need to be so uppity, thinking that I'm above petty criminal suspicion. But that doesn't mean I'm going to run out and get a tattoo and a nose ring. And the shirt? The shirt is definitely staying on.

To host Charles Marshall at your event,
e-mail him at charlesmarshall@kregel.com.